# The Writer's Everything Quarterly

## Essays on Writing from October-December 2019

QJ Martin

# Preface

## October 21st

NaNo Prep for Pantsers
Prepping Without Plotting
Writing Definitions
Developing Your Character
>What is his name?

## October 28th

"What's My Motivation?"
Prologues—The Kiss of Death?
Developing Your Character
>Why was he given his name?
>Does he like his name?
>Does he have any aliases?

## November 4th

*If So, Why? The Ultimate Character Development Guide*
Developing Your Character
>Does he have any nicknames?
>What was the spirit behind his nicknames?
>How does he feel about his nicknames?
>Has he ever tried to change his nickname?

## November 11th

Tracing for Authors
Writing Concepts—Character Arc

*Table of Contents*

How big is his home?

Does anyone else live with him?

What is the condition of the outside of his home?

Crafting Compelling Character Arcs—Black Widow

Writing Definitions

Caricature

Personification

Anthropomorphism

Flanderization

Character Agency

Character Motivation

## December 23rd

The One-Week Author

Writing Concepts—Character Wants

Developing Your Character

What is the condition of the inside of his home?

Does he like his home?

Do others like his home?

Where does he wish he lived?

Crafting Compelling Character Arcs—Iron Man

Writing Definitions

Archetype

Iconic Character

Character Arc

Positive Character Arc

Negative Character Arc

Flat Character Arc

## Bonus Essay—Discovering Inspiration

# Preface

For as long as I can remember, I've loved storytelling. Ever since I discovered that it was possible to actually make a living from creating other worlds, I've wanted to be a writer. Yet it felt like such an impossible and far-off dream. There was simply too much involved. Then, roughly a year and nine months ago, as of the time of this writing, something strange happened.

The desires that had been such a cornerstone of my life for as long as I could remember solidified into a plan of action. I was going to learn the craft and call myself, in no uncertain terms, a writer.

Since then, I've listened to hundreds of hours of podcasts and audiobooks on the writing craft, from *Writing Excuses* to *Helping Writers Become Authors*, from *On Writing* by Stephen King to *Save The Cat! Writes A Novel* by Jessica Brody.

Three-act structure, five-act structure, character archetypes, genres, character arcs, thematic arcs, inciting incidents, wants, needs; I've been nothing short of a sponge for over a year now. I've learned a lot, and I've got a lot to learn.

But if there's one thing that makes humans so unique among the millions of different species that inhabit this world, it's our capacity for language. One person can write their knowledge, wisdom, feelings, and experiences, then another person, across space, time, and cultures can read it, essentially uploading the information directly into their brains. Ten thousand miles away, four thousand years later, it makes no difference.

This is how we grow as a culture, how we improve, how we better ourselves. So, of course, with my studying came the ardent desire to contribute to our ever-growing legacy. In October of 2019, I began publishing a weekly writing magazine titled *The Writer's Everything*. Through its pages, I've aimed to share what I've learned through the lens of my own unique perspective.

The following is a collection of all the articles that appeared in the first three months' issues of *The Writer's Everything*. If you'd like to receive future releases sent directly to your inbox, please feel free to sign up for *The Writer's Everything* newsletter at qjmartin.org/newsletter.

Thank you so much for taking a few minutes out of your

doubtlessly busy life to peruse through this publication. I am so grateful to have you as a reader and, quite soon, a fellow author.

QJ Martin

January 5th, 2020

# October 21st

The following articles were originally published in
*The Writer's Everything*, Issue #001.

# NaNo Prep for Pantsers

This is it. This is the year that you're actually going to do it. You've been wanting to write a novel for the last ten, twenty, or even thirty years of your life, and now you finally have the motivation to make that dream a reality.

When it comes to motivating prospective writers, nothing has had more unmitigated success than the National Novel Writing Month, or NaNoWriMo. I'm sure more than a few of us are counting down the days till November, eagerly looking forward to reaching that 50,000-word goal on the contest's 20th anniversary.

Now, the question is, will you be among the thousands of writers who earn their winner's certificate, or will you fall short? I believe that the answer depends a great deal on how much time and effort you put into preparing for November's arrival.

Do you hear that? That is the sound of millions of PANTSER voices suddenly crying out in terror. Let me start by saying, do I agree?

PANTSER: A writer who does not plan anything out

ahead of time, instead choosing to fly by the seat of their pants.

No.

Do I understand?

Kind of!

I meant to type that I completely understand and sympathize with pantsers, but it didn't sit well with me. That being said, I still want you to do the very best you can this November, and if this magazine can provide you with the boost needed to achieve success, even as a pantser, then I provide that assistance gladly.

That being the case, I've decided to dedicate the inaugural issue of *The Writer's Everything* to you. The following article will focus on things pantsers can do to prepare for NaNoWriMo.

# Prepping Without Plotting

So, what does it take for you, as a pantser, to prepare to succeed in this year's NaNoWriMo competition? How about we start with your day-to-day life.

First, don't plan on going anywhere during NaNoWriMo! As soon as the first of November comes around, you are officially a hermit. You are an introvert. You are a homebody. Tell everyone what you're doing. Tell them about your plan. Make sure they know how important it is for you.

Now, let's say it's not possible to avoid traveling in November. Well, in that case, it's time to start considering what utensils and apps you're going to be using to write down your story.

There are plenty of options available. The first thing you have to decide on is if you want to write your notes LONG-HAND or record them digitally.

> LONG-HAND: Writing that is done by hand with a writing utensil in a notebook or another variety of paper.

If writing with the ol' pen and paper is your modus operandi, then you have countless options to choose from, anywhere from a dollar to a couple dozen bucks. Think about how large you want your notebook to be. Do you need to fit it in your pocket, in your center console, in the drawer of your desk? Or would you rather have as much real-estate as possible, to fill each page to the brim? Do you care about the quality of your paper, or is it all the same in your mind?

Once you decide on a notebook, you also need to choose a writing utensil. Unfortunately, I cannot recommend my favorite pen, namely the Pilot G2, because it tends to smear as I write. I believe that's a problem with most gel pens. Honestly, if I had to recommend any pen, it would ironically enough be the Pentel R.S.V.P. It's one of the cheapest available, but it makes a terrifically clear line. But once again, there are endless options, from cheap to expensive, from ballpoint to fountain.

What if you want to go digital? Well, in that case, you have three options.

First, you can type on a screen. There are endless mobile apps that are simply fantastic for writing, and along with those note-taking tools, you have a wide variety of downloadable keyboards to help you transfer your thoughts to the page at breakneck speed.

If I had to suggest my favorite combination, it would be Evernote with SwiftKey. I'd choose Evernote for its user interface, as well as the ability to log in on my laptop and have instant access to my notes. SwiftKey has been my go-to for years because of its swiping abilities, allowing me to type quite literally as quickly as I can think.

If you're on iOS, however, you can't do better than Scrivener. The mobile version is very close to the capacities of the desktop version, and they have syncing functionality as well.

Second, you can type on a physical keyboard. If this is your preference, I completely sympathize with you. I am personally incapable of developing solid PROSE without the use of a physical keyboard. Luckily, your options for physical typing are incredibly diverse, from tablets with keyboard covers to laptops to desktops.

> PROSE: A communication style utilizing the natural flow of speech, rather than the rhythmic structure of poetry.

Once again, you have your pick of writing software, from Evernote to Scrivener to bibisco to Microsoft Word to Pages to iA Writer. It may take a little time, and a little experimentation, but I have no doubt you can find the perfect app for your process.

Third, you can record your voice and either transcribe the recording to an app later or use transcribing software to do it for you. Personally, I'd only suggest this method if you're performing a task where typing is impossible, such as driving, exercising, or other physical activities. Even then, you need to take care not to put your life in danger just to knock out a couple thousand words.

Now, my final two suggestions to help you to prepare for NaNoWriMo come dangerously close to plotting, but perhaps they will work for you anyway.

What am I referring to? Well, first would be establishing what your SETTING is beforehand. Sure, you don't want to plot your story, but if you give it a little bit of thought, you can still decide on what era and world your story is going to take place in, whether its historical or modern or fantasy or second-world or futuristic or a galaxy far, far away.

SETTING: The time, place, weather, social conditions, or other circumstances under which a story occurs.

*October 21st*

There are all sorts of options open to you. Really, it all depends on what type of genre you want to write in.

And then, the last thing you can do to prepare to succeed in NaNoWriMo is to identify what your POV, your POINT-OF-VIEW, is going to be. You have multiple choices. You can write in first person, "I eat the food," third person, "He eats the food," or the extremely rare second person, "You eat the food." You can also write in present tense, "I eat the food," or past tense, "I ate the food." Knowing what POV you're going to write in ahead of time can save you much hassle and effort when you begin to write your NaNo-winning manuscript.

> POINT-OF-VIEW: The perspective through which a story is being told, or the person who is telling the story.

# Writing Definitions

Like any career or hobby, there's a whole world built around writing that you may just be scratching the surface of. And let's face it, we're not born knowing how to respond if someone on Twitter asks if the MC in your WIP finds the McGuffin, or if it was just a red herring all along.

Well, that's what the Writing Definitions section of this magazine is going to be for. Rather than spending endless hours trying to develop a feel for what all these various terms mean, a few specific terms will be defined with each issue of *The Writer's Everything*.

They will be divided into eight different categories, Character, Plot, Structure, Genre, Narrator, Story Development, Writer, and Business-related terms. I hope that as this magazine continues, these terms can come to be so familiar to you that they become second nature.

# Developing Your Character

*Basic Information > Name*

## What is his name?

Choosing a name is an essential step in the development of your character. A good name can come to embody everything your character is and represents. You can't hear the names Indiana Jones, James Bond, or Darth Vader without immediately picturing the characters, their attributes, and what they stand for.

Sometimes choosing a name can be arbitrary. In *Avatar*, there's no indication that the name Jake Sully has any profound significance.

Sometimes the name itself has significance. In *The Hunger Games*, Peeta's name, as well as that of his country Panem, were chosen because of their connections to the themes of food and bread.

Sometimes a character's name is representative of his nationality or the time period he lives in. In *Captain America: The First Avenger*, Schmidt's name is indicative of the fact that he is a German scientist. In *The Lord of the Rings*, Gandalf's name is a reminder of the fantasy setting he lives in.

Sometimes a character's name is chosen specifically because of his attributes. In *Toy Story*, Woody and Buzz have names directly related to the types of action figures they are. In *Legends of Tomorrow*, Rip Hunter's name is a very tongue-in-cheek reference to his multi-dimensional profession as a hunter of rips in the space-time continuum.

# October 28th

The following articles were originally published in *The Writer's Everything*, Issue #002.

# "What's My Motivation?"

You've heard that it can happen. You know people who have experienced it, and they say it was the greatest thing that ever happened to them. They were writing a novel and an entire section, if not the whole thing, wrote itself.

So what's the secret to being able to experience this amazing occurrence in your writing? Is there one single thing that, if it exists, will cause all the other pieces to fall into place with minimal interference from you, the author?

Perhaps you might think of having a setting. If you're in a galaxy far, far away, the story will just write itself. But will it? Well, why are the people shooting at the other people and trying to destroy their big spaceship? See, now you have to start asking yourself questions, rather than writing your adventure.

Perhaps you might think that you just need to zoom in on the setting, focusing on something more specific. If you choose to write about the American Civil War, then the story will just write itself. But will it? Is your MAIN CHARACTER going to be in the North, or are they going to be in the South? Are there going to be MAJOR CHARACTERS on both sides, or will neither side feature a PRIMARY CHARACTER? Will the story focus on civilians, casualties, or other nations during this tumultuous time in the history of the United States of America?

MAIN CHARACTER: The main character is the central character through whom you experience the story. They are present at major events and are affected by them.

MAJOR CHARACTER: A major character is a character whose presence is necessary for the progression of the story. POV (point-of-view) characters are generally major characters.

PRIMARY CHARACTER: Characters who have major roles in the story. They can include the main character, the protagonist, antagonist, villain, and any character who has a POV in the story.

Perhaps you might think that you need to have your characters established. If you know you're going to be writing about a super-powered mutant, then some aspects of your plot might begin to fall in place. Honestly, I believe you're on the right track.

The specific answer, in my mind, is character motivation. When you know what your character wants and why they want it, then you're in a great position to watch the events of your story unfold before your eyes.

The Rebels want freedom from oppression, and thus they attack the Empire, intending to topple it. The Empire wants complete and total dominance, and thus they build a weapon that is capable of destroying an entire planet in a single blast. The Rebels don't want to die, and thus they attempt to destroy said weapon.

A character that doesn't want anything isn't going to do anything, and a character that doesn't do anything is boring.

If I was a tiny gardener in my own little slice of paradise, I wouldn't go on a year-long journey into hell for no good reason. But if my best friend is making that journey because doing so means that the entire world will be saved from evil, then I would go too, both to help stop that evil and, more importantly, to help my friend stay safe.

As long as you know what your characters want, even if you know nothing else, you're ready to write a novel. In fact, why don't you develop two characters on the fly right now? Give them opposite motivations. Make it impossible for both of them to be simultaneously successful, then see what happens. I bet out of that will come a fun, enjoyable, exciting story.

# Prologues—The Kiss of Death?

There is a sort of stigma in the writing community, especially in certain circles, when it comes to PROLOGUES. We can probably postulate that the premise of this pre-plot problem is, put simply, that prologues are a bait-and-switch.

> PROLOGUE: A section of your novel that is placed before your main story, that generally occurs before the bulk of the novel, and that revolves around separate yet related events.

Most writers agree that a novel must begin with a "hook," something that hooks the reader's attention and makes them want to continue turning page after page. The issue comes when the beginning of your novel is, quite simply, not that interesting.

To solve such an issue, many writers begin their novels with a prologue, something fast-paced and exciting, to serve as the hook of the novel. However, many readers believe that this is a bit of a cheat. They think that you're using characters and settings and time periods that may potentially never appear again to convince your reader to keep turning pages past your boring first chapter.

So the question is, are prologues truly as malevolent as some writers feel they are? Are they the kiss of death for your story?

## The Power of Prologues

As with any other advice, there are nuggets of wisdom found in the suggestion to avoid prologues. You do, in fact, run the risk of disappointing your readers.

What if the characters that you are following are more interesting than your main characters? In that case, your reader will be disappointed when the switch is made. What if the characters that you are following are less interesting than your main characters? In that case, your reader will probably be rather disappointed in the prologue anyway.

The same can be said for plot and setting. And thus, you can see the conundrum we as writers have in this regard. But I don't think we should shy away from including prologues. Prologues can serve one of two purposes, and I believe they must if we are to include them in the opening of our stories.

# Setting The Tone

Picture yourself in a large theater. There's a soda in your left hand, a bag of popcorn in your right, and above you the lights are rapidly dimming. The musical score of the film you're there to watch reaches a crescendo. The camera pans down. There's a planet. We zoom in. The main character is with his uncle walking around a pawn shop, looking through their collection of droids.

He reminds his uncle that the droid they select needs to speak Bocce. His uncle chooses the appropriate models and tells his nephew to clean them up. He whines that he would rather go to the store to buy power converters.

Is this an interesting scene? No, not in the slightest. Yet it's still necessary for establishing Tatooine as a setting, and Luke as a character who is going to develop in a clear arc throughout the rest of the story.

So how do you hook your viewers (readers) if the essential establishing scenes are so bland and ordinary, as they often are?

You include a prologue that sets the tone for the rest of the story. Instead of going straight to the planet, open with a tiny spaceship being pummeled by an immense Star

Destroyer. Have a shootout, followed by a looming, dark, evil knight walking through the destruction.

Does this scene provide us with our main character? No. Does this scene provide us with our setting? No. Would the story still have been comprehensible without this prologue?

I'd argue that it would. Our knowledge of events would be stripped down, becoming equal to that of both Luke and Han, and thus, we would still learn everything as they learn it.

So what is the purpose of this opening prologue? Simply put, it's to set the tone. It helps us to see that this is going to be an epic space adventure, that it's going to be a story of good versus evil, of the weak opposing the strong, and that there're going to be a lot of exciting action scenes to boot.

If *Star Wars IV: A New Hope* did not take place in space, if it did not feature good versus evil, if there wasn't a single dogfight or laser-gun fight in the film, then it would have been that dreaded bait-and-switch of which we referred to earlier.

Simply put, though, there are few, if not none at all, who would have a problem with this prologue the way it was presented in the movie. It hooked us with the promise of what we could expect in that film, and then it made good on that promise.

## Providing Backstory

You go back to that same theater next week. Last week's film got you pumped up. You're looking forward to this next epic movie. The lights dim yet again, and the logo crosses the screen, accompanied by the soft ringing of the string section of the orchestra.

Then strange, short characters appear on the screen, drinking ale and lallygagging around. They're shushed, and an equally short, old man walks up onto the podium in front of them and gives a little speech about turning one hundred and eleven years old.

Is this an interesting scene? It has the potential to be, but it's not inherently so on its own.

After all, we don't know who these characters are. We don't know why they are the focus of this story, and we have no idea what the main conflict of the plot will be. So how do you make sure that the viewers (readers) know what's going on, know what's at stake, and are ready to be fully immersed in this second world?

You include a prologue that establishes the concept of this world, the struggles that the characters may be confronted with, and even background information about the characters themselves.

This is nowhere as necessary as it is in the sci-fi and fantasy genres.

Of course, prologues that are nothing but pure exposition dumps can be weak and undesirable in themselves. At times, writers may choose to circumvent this issue by creating a main character who serves the function of the curious audience. However, that has the potential to be just as clunky. Not every story can have a character who is so purely ignorant of the goings-on of their world without the occasional narrative hiccup.

But a prologue done well can serve to give us the backstory and information that we need to be able to comprehend what is going on in the story, so that we can read the book unhindered by a lack of knowledge.

Once again, if the story of *The Lord of the Rings* did not revolve around elves, dwarves, and humans opposing a dark personification of evil, if the main characters weren't hobbits, and if their characteristics were not essential to the advancement of the plot, then its opening prologues would have been a bait-and-switch.

But how many people did not enjoy the opening of *The Fellowship of the Ring*? How many people thought it was false advertising? Conversely, how many people would have had no idea what was going on if they were not offered this backstory to Middle-Earth, its various races, its oppressive villain, and the hobbits themselves?

There are plenty of ways to write poorly executed prologues. However, rather than vilifying prologues outright, I believe that our focus should be on identifying when they may be necessary and what the elements of a great prologue are. That way we'll know when a prologue would be beneficial to our story, and we'll be able to add skillfully add it to our novel.

No, prologues aren't the kiss of death. Rather, like every other aspect of writing, they require training and finesse. So go write yourself a prologue. Find out how it affects the opening of your story. And don't be afraid to go against the grain.

# Developing Your Character

*Basic Information > Name*

## Why was he given his name?

While some characters' names may be chosen for the reasons listed in last week's issue of *The Writer's Everything*, other characters' names may turn out to be integral to the plot of the story itself. In *Star Wars VII: The Force Awakens*, Ben Solo is so named because of his parents' relationship with Ben Kenobi. In *A Song of Ice and Fire*, bastards receive a last name based on where they live. Jon Snow's name indicates that he is an illegitimate child from a family in the north.

This is even more common in prequels, where we're already familiar with the characters' names, and now the story is offering us a moment of fan service to explain how they received those iconic names. In *Star Trek*, we see that James Tiberius Kirk is named after the fathers of both of his parents. In *Solo: A Star Wars Story*, we see that Han Solo receives his name because he is alone, without anyone to claim as his family.

# Does he like his name?

WHY OR WHY NOT?

Most characters have their names chosen for them at a young age, if not at birth. Needless to say, not every character likes his own name. Some even go as far as to make a deliberate effort to convince their friends and acquaintances to call them by different names. In *Tangled*, the main character chooses to go by Flynn Rider because he thinks that his given name, Eugene, doesn't sound cool. In the *Indiana Jones* series, the main character goes by the nickname Indiana because he likes it better than his given name, Henry Walton Jones.

# Does he have any aliases?

IF SO, WHY?

At times, characters are known by aliases, either in place of, or to a greater extent than, their actual names. In *The Lord of the Rings*, the innkeeper doesn't know Aragorn's real name, yet he knows that people call him Strider. In the DC universe, both Bruce Wayne and Batman are equally well-known names, but few people are aware of the fact that Batman is actually Bruce's crime-fighting alter-ego.

There are usually reasons why characters are known by aliases. In the DC universe, Bruce Wayne goes by Batman to hide his identity and to protect the people he loves. In *Star Wars IV: A New Hope,* Obi-Wan Kenobi goes by Ben so that he won't be outed as the infamous Jedi. In *The Lego Movie,* Wyldstyle changes her name at regular intervals because of her own insecurities.

# November 4th

The following articles were originally published in
*The Writer's Everything*, Issue #003.

# If So, Why? The Ultimate Character Development Guide

If you've read either of the first two issues of this magazine, you may have noticed the section with the title: "Developing Your CHARACTER." (If you haven't, then welcome! I'm glad you're here.) Each week, I include a question or three which I pull out of a list of 850+ character development questions.

> CHARACTER: A person, figure, inanimate object, or animal. Characters guide readers through their stories, helping them to understand plot points and ponder themes.

Originally, I intended to simply post a couple of questions every week, and maybe in a year or two, I would make the entire guide available for purchase. However, I finally came to the decision that I would rather share this guide with the writing community in its entirety than piecemeal it over weeks and months and years.

With that goal in mind, I created a new KICKSTARTER campaign. The way it works is that you, the backers, choose a level that you feel comfortable with, and pledge to spend that much money on this guide.

> KICKSTARTER: A crowd-funding website designed to aid in the development of individual projects by offering rewards in exchange for monetary support.

If the guide is fully funded within the 30 days that I set for the campaign, then your money will be used to put the finishing touches on it and get it out to you on the double.

If it is not fully funded at the end of 30 days, then it will be a failed campaign, and you will not be charged a single penny.

# Not A Pay Wall

Now, this doesn't mean that I am putting my content behind a paywall. I want my contributions to the writing community to be accessible for all aspiring authors, no matter how much they are capable of spending. The "Developing Your Character" section will continue to be made available week by week in this magazine for free.

However, if you have the money, just think how good that hardcover guide would look on your coffee table. If you need some inspiration, cross your legs, put the book in your lap, and flip through it, page by page, question by question, and see what you discover about your character.

## What's The Money For?

Ok, so there are essentially three things that this Kickstarter campaign is intended to be used to fund.

- I need a professionally made cover.
- I need a professional EDIT.

  EDIT: The stage of the writing process where a writer works to improve a draft by correcting errors and making words and sentences clear, precise, and effective.

- I need an ISBN.

Those are three things that time and motivation alone won't manage to provide me with. They are not, strictly speaking, necessary, but if I want my guide to be of the highest quality possible, and I do, then I will need to be able to pay for these common services.

# Don't Answer Them All

While my goal is to make this the most thorough character development guide in existence, I can no doubt imagine many making the argument that such a list of questions would be largely pointless. There's no way you could answer all 850+ questions about each of your primary characters.

However, that's not exactly the point of this guide. The point is to help you to get the creative juices flowing as you contemplate what unique qualities your character could have.

What if you need to have some camaraderie among friends, and you just so happen to see the questions found in this week's issue of *The Writer's Everything*.

*Does he have any nicknames? How does he feel about them?*

Now you're thinking about your character's BACKSTORY. Does he have a nickname? Did his friends give it to him because of his pure awesomeness, or was it a tongue-in-cheek insult? Does he embrace his nickname, or does he do everything within his power to distance himself from it?

BACKSTORY: A narrative history and set of facts and factors that are all chronologically earlier than the narrative of primary interest.

From just a couple of simple questions, you can discover aspects of your character that you never even knew existed.

# The Rewards

There are four different items available for those who support my project on Kickstarter.

One is a digital copy of the guide. Everyone gets that, as long as you spend at least one dollar.

Then there are paperback and hardcover copies of the guide. Those are perfect for sitting back on the couch and conducting some research or looking for some inspiration.

And finally, there's the *If So, Why?* workbook. This is a paperback book containing pages for numerous characters, each one with slots for you to write your answers to as many of the questions as you feel is necessary.

If you would like to support this Kickstarter campaign, simply click the link below. If you would rather not, then there's no need to worry. Just make sure you're subscribed to my newsletter to receive more free content in the future.

Sign up at qjmartin.org/newsletter.

# Developing Your Character

*Basic Information > Name*

## Does he have any nicknames?

Not every character is simply known by his name or alias (both discussed in previous issues). Some go by nicknames, which are either terms of endearment or abbreviated forms of their original names. In the Star Wars franchise, Han, and then by extension everyone else, addresses his copilot as Chewie because it's shorter and easier to say than Chewbacca. In *Ready Player One*, Aech refers to Parzival as Z instead of using his gamer tag whenever he wants to address him.

## What was the spirit behind his nicknames?

Not every nickname is given as a term of endearment. At times, a nickname may be given to a character as an insult, or out of frustration. In *Get Smart*, the other agents call Max a variety of nicknames, such as Maxi Pad, because they dislike him. In *Hey Arnold!*, Helga calls Arnold 'Football

Head' as an insult with the goal of hiding the fact that she is in love with him.

# How does he feel about his nicknames?

Just as not every nickname is given as a term of endearment, not every character always appreciates or is amused by his nicknames. Some come to the point of absolutely hating their nicknames. In *Get Smart*, Max grows highly frustrated by the constant nicknames that the other agents bestow upon him, offering up sarcastic responses to discourage their behavior. In *Big Hero 6*, Wasabi is quite aggravated by the fact that his nickname came from a singular incident of spilling wasabi on his shirt.

# Has he ever tried to change his nickname?

A character may have such strong negative feelings regarding the nicknames his friends have bestowed upon him that he actively works to convince them to refer to him by different nicknames. In *The Big Bang Theory*, Howard makes every effort to try to convince his fellow astronauts to choose the nickname Rocket Man for him. However, they instead elect to call him Fruit Loops due to an embarrassing exchange with his mother over video chat.

# November 11th

The following articles were originally published in
*The Writer's Everything*, Issue #004.

# Tracing for Authors

When it comes to writing, most people have their end goal firmly in mind: sign book deals, get published, sell the rights to Hollywood, move into a mansion, live off the ROYALTIES.

ROYALTIES: Writers that have their works published for sale generally earn a percentage of the money that each copy earns, although at times, magazines and other publishers may pay outright for the story, so as not to owe royalties to the author.

Ok, that may or may not be a little exaggerated, depending on the person. Most of us who have been in the business for any amount of time know that it's an ever more elusive goal. Even so, deep down, we all still want our writing to have the potential to make money.

That being said, now that NaNoWriMo is in full swing, I can't help but think that this is as good of a time as any to discuss writing from another perspective. The perspective of which I speak is writing as an exercise, the sole purpose of which is to enhance your skills.

I like to think of this idea as tracing for authors. I mean think about any other artistic endeavor.

How do you learn to draw? You copy the works of others, perhaps even using tracing paper so that you can absorb every detail of their technique.

Likewise, how do you learn how to be a musician? You recreate the works of others, playing their pieces note by note so that you can learn not only how to play your instrument, but what the salient features of a good piece are.

If you're an actor, how do you learn to hone your craft? You replicate famous scenes from movies and/or well-known pieces of literature, such as Shakespeare's plays, scenes that teach you new the techniques of your craft.

The question now, though, is this: Is there a method for writers to "trace" the work of other writers?

Well, the first issue in this method of creation is that copying someone else's works word-by-word without attribution is, in fact, illegal. It's called PLAGIARISM.

PLAGIARISM: The process of taking the works of another author and attempting to pass them off as your own.

*November 11th*

There is one important detail that it would be good to remember regarding plagiarism: Plagiarism requires you to attempt to publish the writing and pass it off as your own.

That is not to say, though, that you can't copy the writing of others for your own edification in your own notebook or note-taking app.

It is at this point that I want to be clear about one thing, and that is that I am not recommending that you copy the works of other authors word-by-word.

There may be some situations where, in very small quantities, such a tactic could be beneficial to your writing. Maybe you read a paragraph that is masterful in the way it guides you through the VISUALIZATION of a scene, or that conveys the exact emotions of a character in a few short sentences. In such cases, it could be extremely beneficial for you to study the structure of this writing, to find out precisely what makes it so great, and, hopefully, to add those methods to your repertoire.

> VISUALIZATION: The method of creating a distinct and clear mental image through the use of the written word.

There are, however, other ways to trace the work of others.

Let's look at a few of them.

# Characters and Settings

The first aspect of writing that you can trace from other authors is their characters and settings.

It can be very beneficial for those who are not experienced in the techniques of world-building and character development to work within the sandboxes of other authors. In that way, you can learn how to work with well-thought-out, developed characters and settings and, at the same time, you can come to understand what your characters and settings need to carry you through an entire story.

The thing about this method of tracing is that you can, in fact, PUBLISH your finished works online, albeit for free, and thousands do just that every day. This sort of writing is known as "fan fiction", and these works have a large following online. Posting your fan fiction on websites such as Wattpad can allow you to have your writing read and assessed by those who know exactly what makes a great story and who can tell you what you've done well and what you could stand to improve on.

PUBLISH: Distributing literature so that others may read it. This includes traditional book publishing, self-publishing, and publishing on blogs and websites such as Wattpad.

## Tone and Concepts

The second aspect of writing that you can trace from other authors is their tone and concepts.

If you love *James Bond* stories, then maybe you can try your hand at writing about the international adventures of a super spy. If you love *Star Wars*, maybe you can try your hand at writing an ensemble story with a "chosen one" and magical powers or a space-western complete with shady characters and train robberies.

This manner of tracing is the greatest choice to provide you finished product that is your sole creative possession. There is no copyright on the concept of spies, nor is there a copyright on the ideas of magical powers or space cowboys. As long as you develop your own stories and characters, the result will be a piece of fiction that you will be free to do with as you please.

# Plot and Story Beats

The third aspect of writing that you can trace from other authors is their plot and story beats.

This can be incredibly helpful if you have difficulty developing your own plots or even if you are just unsure what should happen next in a story with a plot of your own.

Really, you'd be surprised how often writers copy the plots of other authors. Think about the story of an orphaned young man living with his aunt, uncle, or both, who discovers he has an amazing inherent ability, and he needs to save the world from a dark lord. Several stories fit that plot, including *Star Wars IV: A New Hope*, the *Harry Potter* series, *The Lord of the Rings*, and *Eragon*.

The question of how much is too much when it comes to tracing the plot of another story is nebulous at best. No one accuses *Harry Potter* of being a rip-off of *Star Wars*, although they share many similarities. On the other hand, some feel that *Eragon* contains such blatant plagiarism from both *Star Wars* and *The Lord of the Rings* that it should not be considered an original work.

What about story beats? Perhaps you're writing a police investigation. It's more likely than not that you do not have any personal experience with the steps that police officers take when investigating a crime. On the flip side, it's incredibly likely that you have read or watched a piece of media that contained such investigations and from that media you can have at least a base idea of what steps are involved and what obstacles may arise.

Is the process of tracing the works of other authors a waste? Not necessarily. Every writer is going to start as an amateur. And every writer is going to need to write for quite a while before their work is worthy of being sold. The question is, will you use that opportunity to learn valuable lessons in your methodology as a writer, or will you not?

And, of course, there's always the possibility that you can develop your traced work into a work of your own. *Fifty Shades of Grey*, regardless of its merits as a novel, famously originated as a *Twilight* fan fiction. So get tracing, get writing, and update me on your progress.

# Writing Concepts—Character Arc

A character arc is, essentially, the transformation of a character over the course of the story. Character arcs are used to make your characters interesting and dynamic, as well as to add a sense of meaning to the story.

Not every character has to have an arc. Some characters may only be present in the story for one or two chapters or may otherwise not be affected by the events of the story. Other characters have what is called a flat character arc, in which the person they are at the beginning and the person they are at the end are fundamentally the same. In such cases, they often cause change in those around them instead. Think of Captain America in *Captain America: The Winter Soldier* for an example of a flat character arc.

For characters who do change over the course of the story, there are two options for their development. They will either have a positive character arc, in which the state of the character at the end of the story is an improvement upon their state at the beginning of the story, or a negative character arc, in which the state of the character at the end of the story is worse than it is at the beginning.

An example of a positive character arc would be that of Sam Worthington's character Jake Sully and his development over the course of *Avatar*.

An example of a negative character arc would be Sam Worthington's more recent role in the Netflix film *Fractured*.

# Developing Your Character

*Basic Information > Age*

## What is his age?

The age of your character can have far-reaching implications in your story. It can affect his levels of knowledge and experience, his naivety, and/or his ability to perform such functions as driving, buying tobacco, alcohol, pornography, or getting into strip clubs and mature-rated movies. In *Home Alone*, the fact that the main character is left by himself is significant because he is only eight years old and has little to no experience with the responsibilities of adulthood. In *Star Wars V: The Empire Strikes Back*, Yoda's wisdom is substantially greater than that of any other character, since he is well over 800 years older than they are.

## What is his birthday?

Knowing the date of your character's birthday can be helpful as you organize the details of your story. If you have a COMING-OF-AGE story with the main character buying alcohol, you'll want to make sure that they're either old enough to do so or have taken the steps necessary to fake their age. In *Titanic*, they attempt to discover the exact age of Rose Dewitt so that they can determine if her claim of being a passenger on the Titanic is feasible or not. In *X-Men: Dark Phoenix*, Eric Lehnsherr is 62 years old, having been born in 1930. However, the actor portraying him, Michael Fassbender, is nearly two decades younger, at 42 years of age during the release of the film.

> COMING-OF-AGE: A story that focuses on the mental and emotional growth of a character as they transition from youth into adulthood. The character may have a great influence on the world around them (*The Hunger Games*) or they may not (*Lady Bird*).

## What does he do to celebrate his birthday?

What a character chooses to do on his birthday can strongly influence many events throughout the story. In *The Lord of the Rings*, Bilbo organizes a party to celebrate his eleventy-first birthday, inviting hundreds of friends and relatives. In *Star Trek: The Next Generation*, Worf prefers to be alone on his birthday, participating in quiet meditation rather than having a party with his crew-mates present.

# November 18th

The following articles were originally published in *The Writer's Everything*, Issue #005.

# Insert Character Development Here

When I was a kid, I loved developing stories. I always pictured each and every SCENE of my epic narrative in my mind, as if they were playing on the big screen at the local theater. Well, every scene except for one type: those of character development.

> SCENE: A unit of story structure in which either action, dialogue, or both takes place. Scenes generally only occur in one location, or during one conversation. The end of a scene is called a scene break.

I had no idea how to develop them. I didn't even know where to start. I knew what the types of scenes I was looking for were. I knew that there was character development going on between Han Solo and Leia Organa when they were stranded together in the Millennium Falcon. But in my stories, starting from scratch, I was worse than clueless.

I used to write a title at the top of the page at certain points in my story, where I knew the "character development" beats needed to go. It would say *(Insert Character Development Here).* It would then be followed by roughly five blank pages.

What belonged in those blanks? I had the rough impression that there needed to be talking. I needed to zoom in on the characters and their motivations. But I had no idea what made high-quality character development, or how long those scenes needed to be.

You might ask, though, is character development really that important for your story? As a matter of fact, it is an essential aspect of storytelling. Sure, you could have ONE-DIMENSIONAL characters with no goals, no aspirations, and no desires. But you have to ask yourself, would the stories of such characters be compelling? Can you root for a character to win the day if you don't even know who they are, what their history is, or what drives them?

> ONE-DIMENSIONAL: A character that either lacks depth or fails to develop and evolve throughout a story. An intentionally one-dimensional character may be used to highlight a particular, usually negative, trait.

On top of that, if you don't establish the motivations for a character, then who's to say that they would do anything at all when presented with the events of the story? If John Doe doesn't have something to live for when the zombie apocalypse arrives, then he's not going to struggle against unbearable odds to stay alive. In fact, if he really has nothing to live for, it's more likely he will simply end his existence rather than fight for it.

So what does it take for you to develop your characters? How do you make sure that they have the proper motivations, and how do you make sure that they're dynamic, constantly evolving?

# 1. Do Your Research

The first thing that is required for quality character development is a starting point for your characters. You need to develop them to the greatest extent possible so that you know exactly who they are from the get-go.

If you want your characters to evolve, to be motivated by the INCITING INCIDENT, and to be changed by the CLIMAX of the story, then you need to have that starting point firmly established.

INCITING INCIDENT: An event that launches the action of the story, usually by drastically impacting the life of the primary characters and moving them to action.

CLIMAX: The point in a story where the rising action or tension of the second act reaches its peak, or highest point, and which leads to falling action and the denouement.

So, what does this require? Well, there are many different options for developing your characters. Countless websites and guidebooks are available with the intention of walking you through the process, with questions as varied as what their history is, what their social and economic conditions are, and what their physical attributes are.

My upcoming ebook, *If So, Why? The Ultimate Character Development Guide,* will contain 850 questions along with descriptions and explanations of each one. The purpose of questions like these isn't to detail every single aspect of your character's history and life, down to how many times they shake it when using the restroom. The purpose is to get to know who your character really is, what drives them, and what makes them unique. The purpose is to open your mind to the possibilities that this blank slate that is your character presents you with.

The question is, how many of these categories are essential

to the development of your character? The answer: whichever ones give you the greatest insights into how your character thinks and how they developed as human beings.

Physical attributes, questions such as, "What color are their eyes?" or, "How tall are they?" obviously won't be as important to their development as questions like "What was their economic situation growing up?" and "Were either of their parents abusive?"

But don't turn this recommendation into a rule. Any abnormalities in the appearance of a character in comparison to that of the fellow youths they grow up with can cause insecurities and inferiority complexes or, on the flip side, extreme privilege, pride, and vanity.

So be sure to give plenty of thought to the questions that are of the greatest importance for your specific character. How can you identify them? The most important thing you need to do is think about your plot.

For example, in *Avatar*, Jake Sully needs to be compassionate and caring if he's going to give up his old life and accept the new one that friendship with the Na'vi offers him. So that means that he has to be dissatisfied with his current life. There has to be something on Pandora for him which humanity is no longer able to offer him. In other words, he can't be rich and well-to-do, and he can't be satisfied with the hand he's been dealt.

In *Iron Man*, Tony Stark needs to be incredibly smart if he's going to be able to develop his suit, and he has to be egotistical and self-centered if he's going to have room to grow as a character by learning to care about others and sacrifice himself for them.

Can you develop characteristics that are not directly related to the motives of the character, nor to their inner self? Of course you can. But it might be better if you don't put too much effort into coming up with them right out the gate. You'll be able to discover plenty of insignificant and mundane details about your character as you write your story.

It's reasonable enough to assume that when the writers of the first *Thor* movie were establishing the details for their eponymous magical hero, a love of coffee was nowhere to be found in their notes. No doubt, it wasn't until they wrote the scene in the diner that they realized the comedic potential of that aspect of his character. It's not an essential detail, but it made for a great scene, and it fit the character's personality.

# 2. Plot Your Character Arc

Now that you have the starting point for your character, the next step you have to take is to plan out what effects the events of the story are going to have on them. This will help you to understand which moments in your story are significant, and thus allow you to identify where to put your focus so as to fully capitalize on their character-developing potential.

These moments of evolution that your character experiences throughout the story come to be known collectively as a "character arc." We discussed the general concept of character arcs in Issue #004 of this magazine. Basically, the character arc is the transformation of a character over the course of the story.

There are three different types of character arcs: positive character arcs, negative character arcs, and flat character arcs. The question is, do you want your character to end in a better (*positive*) position than when they started, a worse (*negative*) position than when they started, or do you want them to be the same (*flat*) as when they started?

Characters that are already heroic and selfless at the beginning of the story, as well as characters that are classified as anti-heroes, or even villains, may not be significantly changed by the plot of the story. Captain America in *Captain America: The Winter Soldier* and Indiana Jones in *Raiders of the Lost Ark* are two examples of characters with flat character arcs.

In that case, your character development will be limited to zooming in on them as individuals and showing what the standards and morals they hold dear are, and perhaps what caused them to be so resolute in the first place.

On the other hand, characters that develop positive traits, becoming better human beings by the end of the story, as well as those who become worse, offer many opportunities for character development that aren't just limited to the establishment of their characters.

# 3. Identify Key Events

There are going to be key events over the course of the story that you will discover while plotting your character and story arcs. As you find them, you'll realize that these are the points where you need to write your story as if viewed from under a magnifying glass, if not a microscope, to show exactly how the characters are developing in these significant moments.

*November 18th*

Tony Stark is selfish and self-centered. He doesn't care what is done with his weapons. Then he's attacked, nearly killed by his own missile. We see the reaction on his face. If this was a written story, his thought process about the significance of this event would be clearly on display. He realizes that he's not untouchable and that it matters what is done with his weapons.

Then Tony Stark makes his first genuine friend, someone who he lets in past his rough, selfish exterior, someone who selflessly sacrifices himself for Tony. That death is a life-altering event for Stark, and thus, we zoom in on him and his feelings, the tragic loss he experiences, and we know that it's going to come to define him down the road.

Following that loss, Tony Stark, with his idealism and sensibilities renewed, is presented with the fact that his weapons are still being sold to and used by terrorists. He now knows that he has a responsibility to do something about it, because his name is on those weapons, just as it was on the missile that nearly killed him. He can no longer stand idly by, so he builds his Iron Man suit and takes the fight to them.

You need to identify the major life-altering events of your own story as well. What are the most significant changes that occur to your character, and when do they take place? When you get to these moments, be sure that you really zoom in on them, and don't allow anything to to fly under the radar.

So do your research. Plot your character arcs. Identify your most important events. Once you know where they are, don't be afraid to write a little note in your MANUSCRIPT that says *(Insert Character Development Here)*. There's nothing wrong with that, in spite of my earlier antidote. Just don't forget about filling it in down the road.

> MANUSCRIPT: Any copy of your novel during the writing or editing process, up until actual publication. Authors often send their manuscripts to publishers in the hopes of getting a book deal.

# Writing Concepts— Antagonist

The force that stands in opposition to the protagonist or major characters of an ensemble story, bringing conflict to the plot.

An antagonist can be a person. Such a character is generally known as a villain, although that nomenclature insinuates that they have ill intentions. An antagonist, however, can have the best of intentions, and may even be doing the right thing if you take into consideration their circumstances alone, but their actions stand in the way of those that the protagonist needs to take.

Animals and objects can serve the function of antagonists in a story. While it might not always be correct to refer to them as antagonists, they can safely be called antagonistic forces. For example, in *Twister* and *The Perfect Storm*, inclement weather serves as the antagonistic force against which the main characters struggle. In *Jaws*, *Sharknado*, *The Shallows*, *The Meg*, and countless other films, sharks serve as the antagonistic force, and the main characters must fight against their animalistic urges to hunt and kill.

In superhero stories, the antagonist is often "defeated" in a climactic battle. In other stories, there may simply be a moment where the main character proves the antagonist wrong or exceeds their expectations.

# Developing Your Character

*Basic Information > Age*

## What do others do to celebrate his birthday?

What others choose to do on a character's birthday can be just as influential to the plot of the story as the choices of the character himself. In *Star Trek: The Next Generation*, Worf's shipmates in an alternate reality choose to forgo Worf's preferences, throwing him a surprise party in spite of his dislike for such occasions. In *Sixteen Candles*, Samantha eagerly looks forward to receiving a surprise party for her birthday, but her family ends up forgetting all about it and she has to occupy her time with other activities. In *The Amazing Spider-Man 2*, neither Max Dillon's mother nor his boss remembers his birthday, and because of that, he is forced to work overtime and suffers a tragic accident, transforming into the super-powered Electro.

## How does he feel about his current

# age?

Age plays a strong role in both character motivations and outlooks on life. A character may choose a path of inaction with the belief that he still has plenty of time left to achieve his goals later. Or a character may make many inadvisable choices because he is 'still young,' or because he wants to achieve the items on his bucket list before he is too old to do so. In *The Lord of the Rings*, Bilbo Baggins realizes that he is getting up in age and decides that he wants to go on one last adventure before he dies. In *Star Trek II: The Wrath of Khan*, James Kirk realizes that without command of the Enterprise his life lacks purpose, and he will quickly become a relic just like his collection of antiques.

# Does he wish he was a different age?

IF SO, WHY?

Often, the opinion that a character holds for his age is directly related to the choices he makes in a given situation. In *Bridge to Terabithia*, Jesse Aarons attempts to act like he's much older and more mature than he actually is in an attempt to earn the affections of his teacher, Ms. Edmunds.

# Does his age influence the way he's treated?

The age of a character can have a substantial effect on the way others perceive and treat him. Children may be seen as immature and irresponsible, while older ones may be looked down on as senile and frail. On the flip side, children may be looked up to as intelligent and adaptable, while older ones may be held in high honor for their wisdom and experience. In *Star Wars I: The Phantom Menace*, the Jedi Council does not want to approve the training of Anakin because they believe he is already too old to begin such a rigorous journey. In *Star Wars II: Attack of the Clones*, Padmé looks down on Anakin's position as a Jedi because of his youth, choosing on at least one occasion to disregard his recommendations in favor of her own. In *Ender's Game*, young children are gathered and trained as soldiers because they have a greater capacity for creative problem solving than adults.

# Cinematic Storytelling— Subverting Expectations

There's a concept that is becoming more and more commonplace in entertainment, in a world where a trailer can't drop, an episode can't air, and a sequel can't be announced without thousands of enthralled fans dissecting every iota of material they've been offered, postulating every potential twist and turn in the upcoming narrative, and publishing their findings online for the rest of the world to share in their excitement. That concept is that subverting expectations is the key to great writing.

Writers, directors, and producers believe that the only solution for developing quality entertainment is to write a conclusion that no one in their respective fandoms has ever predicted. They think that if it's a surprise to the audience, that will automatically make it amazing. That reasoning, of course, is not only fundamentally flawed, but it brings into painful focus the lack of merit that said individuals have as writers, at the very least in regard to the works in which they make this creative choice.

The following is a list of four reasons why subverting

expectations is not the be-all, end-all of quality storytelling. Before we get into it, though, I want to make it clear that this is a topic that I am quite passionate about. It boils my blood when directors and writers justify the poor choices they make in their stories with such expressions as, "People would have been mad no matter what we did," or "They're only upset because it wasn't the answer they wanted."

I do not, however, intend this article to ruffle anyone's feathers, nor to insult those who enjoyed some of the recent examples of subverting expectations that we've seen on both the big screen and the small screen. I believe that storytelling is an art, and for the most part, I believe that there is a right way to do things and a wrong way. These four reasons are simply my explanation for why I think subverting expectations for the sake of subverting expectations is the wrong way.

## 1. The biggest surprise is rarely the greatest choice for storytelling.

If your story is about a neck-and-neck political race, the most surprising result, for the sake of argument, could be that a big flying saucer comes out of the sky and abducts the protagonist's opponent, allowing him to win the race by default. As I said, that would be the most surprising result, but it would in no way, shape, or form transform the story into an amazing work of art.

On the other hand, if the main character discovers that his opponent is a spy working to take down the government from the inside, and there were hints that this was the case all along, then you have something that you can just about call a good story, and that is the case whether your audience predicted it or not.

In the same way, having your main heroine go mad and be killed after years of character development and foreshadowing that depicted her as level-headed and sensible might be the most surprising choice available to the writer of a TV show, but it doesn't mean that it's high-quality story-telling.

## 2. You insult the intelligence of your audience.

Whether the writers like it or not, many popular movies and television shows have fanbases composed of highly intelligent, highly skilled individuals. Said geniuses can easily predict the ending of their series of choice, whether based on a gut feeling, the process of elimination, or the very obvious breadcrumbs that were laid out for them to follow in the first place.

If a writer chooses to do the complete opposite of what every one of his IP's fans has guessed, just for the sake of surprise, it's nothing less than an insult to the intelligence of those fans. It's as if the writer is saying, "Oh, so you figured out what I had planned all along? Well, I'm just going to change it. I bet you didn't see that coming! Not so smart now, are you?"

If everyone and their mother is guessing who the heroine's parents are, and the writer decides to say that they were nobody, in spite of all the foreshadowing and insinuation to the contrary, just for the sake of choosing an option that no one among the fanbase has predicted, then the writer is essentially saying that the combined intelligence of all the members of his audience is too paltry to be able to accurately predict the ending to his movie, and he's going to make sure of that if it's the last thing he does.

# 3. A surprise resolution is only satisfying if you're given the tools to see it coming.

There's a detail in story-telling that transforms your tales from mindless entertainment to layered and nuanced works of art. That detail, which I've mentioned already, is called foreshadowing.

A high-quality, satisfying ending is one that you can analyze after the fact and realize it was hinted at all along. Whether you connected the dots or not, once the big reveal is over, you ought to be able to say, "I should have seen that coming."

And believe me, if you've done your job well, if you've done adequate foreshadowing, there will be people who see your ending coming. That's not the sign of a bad story, but an indication of good, high-quality writing.

# 4. Your audience should be rewarded, not condemned.

Movies, television, books, video games, etc., are all, when it comes down to it, produced for our entertainment. The viewers are supposed to be able to enjoy them, and that requires providing them with the best experience possible.

While some may argue that it limits creative freedom, shouldn't most works of entertainment strive to make the audience, the ones who make their very existence possible, pleased with their endings?

If they have stuck with you as the creator through thick and thin, if they've watched and shared and posted about and gone to conventions and gotten autographs and all-around geeked out over the subject that you are writing, why would you choose to self-destruct your own story, rather than take it in a direction that someone, somewhere, has predicted at some point?

# December 6th

The following articles were originally published in
*The Writer's Everything*, Issue #006.

# The Economization of Intellectual Property

Nearly every person who calls themselves a writer has one dream objective that's always hovering right in the back of their minds: they want to be able to make a living off of their writing. It's the ever-elusive act of quitting our day job which we are all actively striving for.

The thing is, though, that the majority of us are far from putting in our two weeks' notice. Factor in the responsibilities of daily life, the cost of food and board, the act of caring for family members, and much more, and we're left with the painfully unfortunate situation of having very little time to be able to dedicate to our dream job.

If you are part of that majority, the majority that doesn't include Stephen King and J.K. Rowling, then you know just how important it is to make every effort count with your writing. But is there a way to go beyond that? Is there a way to economize our creativity, to allow our hand-crafted words and hard-fought grammatical victories to pull double duty, triple duty, or more?

# The Key

The key to economizing your creativity, to get more value out of your writing than its simple face value is to remember that when you write something, it is yours. Those words, in that order, are your INTELLECTUAL PROPERTY, and until or unless you sign a contract to part with your IP, you can use those words in any way that you want.

> INTELLECTUAL PROPERTY: Creations of the mind, such as inventions, artistic and literary works, designs, and the like. They are items to which their creators have the rights, and which they can patent, copyright, or trademark.

What that means is that the blog post you wrote last week, the one you thought was pure genius, can become a series of tweets. The movie you watched last night wasn't a waste of time, because now you have a movie review on your blog, a video review on YouTube, and your glowing recommendation on Facebook. The dream journal in which you record your nightly adventures first thing every morning can become the inspiration for a short story, a novel, or a memoir.

There are over seven billion people in this world. The

chances are strong that there is someone somewhere who, upon discovering you, would become your biggest fan, would read everything that you write, and would impatiently demand for more.

Not everyone, however, is going to find you on Twitter. Not everyone is going to read your blog. Not everyone is going to watch your YouTube videos, listen to your podcast, or watch your live stream. But each of those avenues of distribution affords you the opportunity to reach a greater and greater audience.

You never know how much interest you'll garner through the varied distributions of your intellectual property. Perhaps someone will find you on YouTube, love your video essays, and seek you out on Kindle or Audible. Perhaps someone will keep up with your tweets for weeks, finally notice that pinned tweet on your profile, and become a rabid fan of your amazing podcast.

Of course, not every tweet is worthy of a YouTube video. Not every blog post is worthy of a live-stream event. So, the question we're left with is, how can we identify the projects that have the greatest potential to be economized, projects that we know will still be valid and meaningful long after we write them.

# Planning Ahead

If you want to economize your intellectual property, you must start by identifying topics that you can write about that will translate well to different mediums. For example, I have a (rather inactive) YouTube account in which I critique and fix movies and TV shows based on, above all else, their story-telling merits.

There are plenty of people who seek out reviews and discussions about their favorite movies. So of course, these videos would make great material for a blog. If there's a lesson that I extracted from the movie that aids in the development of storytellers, then those lessons would make perfect articles for a magazine intended to help storytellers, such as, say, this one.

# Economizing Hobbies

Hobbies are just as ripe for economization as anything if you're clever about it. Say you love to go shopping. In that case, make a live stream where you're unpacking all of the items that you bought, make a YouTube video where you review each of them, and then send out a couple of tweets recommending the greatest items in your haul.

Say you like to collect certain objects, such as coins, stamps, shot glasses, or spoons. As you collect those items, make a tiny little note about the situation under which you bought or found each of them. The next thing you know, you have a blog series and an upcoming Kindle book discussing your journey to assemble the greatest coin or ugly sweater collection in the world.

## Lean Into Your Interests

As you contemplate ways that you can economize your creativity, keep in mind that the best subjects to write about are going to be ones that interest you. If you're an expert craftsman, but you hate writing how-to guides for power tools, it's not going to magically become more enjoyable if you also decide to create a podcast explaining how to use power tools.

The things you write should always be those that pique your interest, but that is even more the case, even more essential, if you're going to be revisiting those works again and again in different forms.

When you're writing, your goal is to try to elicit certain emotional responses from your readers. If you're not excited about what you're discussing, if it isn't a topic that makes you giddy, and if every article or tweet is a chore, then you're not going to be able to draw your readers in and allow them to have the sort of emotional response that keeps them coming back for more. That is equally true even when it is, in fact, a topic that they themselves have interest in.

While hundreds of thousands of individuals, if not more, claim the title of writer, much time and energy is required to really make a go of this profession. Thankfully, with a little planning, and a dash of creativity, your words can take you twice as far, if not further, towards your goal of being a successful writer.

# Writing Concepts—Genre Conventions

GENRE conventions are the story elements that are common, if not unique, to the genre in which an author chooses to write their story.

> GENRE: The style in which a story is written, or the category in which the story fits. Genres are used for indexing books in libraries and bookstores, and for readers to quickly discover novels that fit their interests.

While a dozen writers may have the same idea for a novel, it's up to each individual to choose how they want to tell it. A large part of that involves the genre which the author chooses for their book.

The same story, such as that of a computer system successfully achieving self-awareness, could be told as a highly intellectual psychological thriller (*Ex Machina*), a high-octane action film (*The Terminator*), an action-oriented murder mystery (*I, Robot*), or a heart-warming but potent character DRAMA (*A.I. Artificial Intelligence*).

DRAMA: A genre of writing that contains conflict of characters, and is conveyed through dialogue between the characters, in either prose or verse form.

Every genre is defined by different and unique characteristics and events. These genre conventions have developed over decades, if not centuries. As readers and watchers consume hundreds of stories in their favorite genres, they come to recognize, and even expect, certain things from those stories.

A romantic comedy will almost always have the couple get into a major argument just pages before realizing the truth about each other and running back into their open arms.

A 'whodunit' will almost always have an ensemble cast packed full of colorful individuals, each one with a long and storied past filled to the brim with connections to the murder victim.

Genre conventions are not set in stone. No author is obligated to write a STORY BEAT simply because it's common in the types of stories they are writing. A middle ground must be found between fulfilling reader expectations and creating a DERIVATIVE WORK.

STORY BEAT: The individual points of action that occur throughout a novel. The story beats are usually all interlinked or related to each other, and together, they form the story.

DERIVATIVE WORK: A work that includes major elements from previously created, original works, transformed, modified, or adapted into a second, separate work.

# Developing Your Character

*Basic Information > Age*

## Does he enjoy getting older, or does he dread it?

Some characters welcome the passage of time with open arms, as it comes with newfound freedom and abilities. Others dread old age. In *The Bucket List,* Edward Cole writes a list of activities that he wants to participate in before he dies, and soon engages in a race against the clock to check them all off before lung cancer takes his life. In *Interview with a Vampire*, Claudia hates the fact that she's stuck in the eternal form of a young girl, wishing instead that she could mature and become a grown woman.

*Basic Information > Location*

## Where does he live?

The location where your character lives can have a large role to play in the plot of your story. In *Spider-Man*, Peter

Parker lives in New York City, which puts him near Oscorp Laboratories, where he is bitten by a radioactive spider and receives his superpowers. His presence among skyscrapers also facilitates his capacity to travel by swinging from building to building, an ability that would be useless in a rural farming community. In *The Village*, the village that the main characters live in is an essential aspect of the plot, and the truths behind its existence are major reveals both to the main character and the audience.

## Does he own, rent, squat, or live with someone else?

The question of whether a character owns, rents, or stays on another individual's property, with or without permission, can reveal a great deal about both his social status and aspects of his personality. In *Batman Begins*, Bruce Wayne lives in a mansion, which demonstrates both his extreme wealth and privileged position among the Gotham City elite. In *Spider-Man 2*, Peter Parker lives in a cheap, run-down apartment which he can barely manage to afford as it is.

## Does his location affect the way he

# sees himself?

IF SO, WHY?

The location where a character lives can have a deep effect on the character's opinion of himself, for better or worse. In *Arrow*, Malcolm Merlyn is a wealthy businessman living in a rich neighborhood in Starling City, which makes him feel superior to those who live in the city's slums, called the Glades. In *The Lord of the Rings*, the citizens of Gondor feel great pride over the fact that they live directly in front of Mordor and are personally responsible for keeping Sauron's forces at bay.

# Cinematic Storytelling—Differentiating an Ensemble Cast

There are very few writing choices as risky as creating a novel with an ENSEMBLE CAST. So much could go wrong, especially for the beginning writer. Yet, if done right, the rewards are more than equal to the challenge.

> ENSEMBLE CAST: A cast including numerous characters, usually all of whom, or at least the majority of whom, function as main characters in the story, as opposed to a story with a single protagonist.

The question is, though, what is the secret to creating a satisfying ensemble cast?

## Unique Characters

The key, in my opinion, is to give each character at least one major, unique characteristic.

For example, think of *The Lord of the Rings*. The story is set in a fantasy world that none of the readers can directly relate with. As such, it would be very easy for the characters to blend in with each other.

Four tall characters that live a long time? Ok. But do these characters all come off as the same?

## Aragorn

Aragorn is a talented swordsman.

## Gandalf

Gandalf is a wise and powerful wizard.

## Legolas

Legolas is an exceptional archer.

## Arwen

Arwen is willing to give up immortality for Aragorn.

Of course, we know that each of these characters holds a

unique position in our memory. But they were also much easier to relate to. What about characters that aren't so easy to relate to, such as the four little hobbits?

## Frodo

Frodo is self-sacrificing and brave.

## Samwise

Samwise is loyal to a fault.

## Merry

Merry is a troublemaker with a deep-seated sense of duty and honor.

## Pippin

Pippin is clumsy and brash, choosing to act before he thinks.

These four characters could have easily blended together and become indistinguishable from each other, but that's not the case. While I might argue that Merry and Pippin were not necessarily easy to tell apart in *The Fellowship of the Ring*, even they eventually developed characteristics that stood out firmly from each other. Compare that with *The Hobbit*. There are thirteen dwarves in this story, and in the book, they are nearly indistinguishable. While the movie adaptations did make efforts to give them unique qualities, it didn't help that they all had names that rhymed with each other or simply blended together in a list.

What if the entire cast is made of preteen youths? Well, think of Stephen King's *It*. Read off the following list of words and tell me if every character doesn't immediately pop into your head as clear as day:

- Writer
- Architect
- Voice-Actor
- Hypochondriac
- Historian
- Accountant
- Designer

That's not to mention their physical characteristics, such as stutterer, overweight, female, Jewish, or their interests, like birdwatching, smoking, etc. The point is, each character has multiple unique aspects that help them to stand out among what could have potentially been an identical cast of young children.

## Try It Out

If you're writing a novel with multiple main characters, then grab a piece of paper, or your favorite note-taking app, and put each of their names as a heading. Now try to give each of them one or two unique characteristics.

That doesn't mean that they can't all have something in common. For example, they could all love D&D, but one of them could be obsessed with writing the adventures, and another could love to do voices, and another could always be quick to run into things without thinking, with the whole group suffering the consequences.

With a little bit of effort, you can develop a wide variety of colorful, interesting, and above all, memorable characters for your novel.

# December 16th

The following articles were originally published in
*The Writer's Everything*, Issue #007.

# Taking A Break—How Long Is Too Long?

No matter how eager you are as a writer, no matter how many ideas you have, or how grand your visions of your career are, there will almost inevitably come a time when you need to cut free from the word count goals and get a little R&R.

Now, I know what you're thinking. You don't want to take a break. You don't want to lose your momentum. You're afraid that you might not get back into the groove, that days will become months and months will become years.

That is not, in fact, an invalid concern. Just like with a vehicle, it takes more effort to get going from a dead stop than it does to coast along at 65. However, sometimes we need to get out and stretch our legs and, above all, refuel so that we can continue on our journey.

The question then is, how do you know when you need to take a break? Once you put the pen or keyboard down, how long can you leave it sitting on the desk before it becomes too long? Of course, there is no one black-and-white answer to this question, an answer that will fit every writer and their methods perfectly. But there are things that we can all keep in mind to help us to gauge when we should pick our writing utensils up again and get back to the grind.

## Gaining Objectivity

When you're wading through an endless forest of words, it's possible to get lost, to lose sight of the big picture for the trees. If you start to feel like the endgame of your writing is getting muddled in your mind's eye, then perhaps a break is exactly what you need.

Taking a day, week, or even a month off can help to give you a fresh perspective on the projects you're working on. If you were facing a challenge that you saw no way around, a steel wall of writer's block, then taking that time away from the project could help you to reorganize your thoughts. Sometimes the solutions to our problems come exactly when we stop thinking about them.

## Refilling Your Creativity

Even if you aren't, per se, having trouble with your writing, the act of taking a break can still be beneficial to you.

Creating an artistic expression is like writing with an ink pen. You can write and write and write with no problem, but when you least expect it, your ink runs out.

Your job as a writer requires you to perform activities to refill your creativity just as much as it requires you to write. Creativity is essential to the writing process, and if you use it all up, it can lead to difficulty writing and, even worse, discouragement.

So, what can you do to recharge your creativity? One of the most important things is to take in more than you put out. This requires that you enjoy the creations of other artists, such as music, poems, short stories, novels, television shows, and movies.

Now, you might scoff at this idea for various reasons. Perhaps you don't enjoy taking in some, or all, of these art forms. Or perhaps you're concerned that if you immerse yourself in someone else's work, it will alter the voice of your work. Really, though, there are more potential benefits than risks with taking in media.

First, it provides you with memories and experiences of aspects of existence that you may have never gained in your own life. While I'll never be a bank robber, of course, I can tell the story of one with at least a passing resemblance to real life, simply because I've seen bank robbers depicted in films and television.

Second, it helps you to learn more about your writing craft through osmosis. As you read a book, you might wonder at the choice of words, the method of describing scenes, or the point-of-view in which an author chooses to write. This will almost inevitably transfer into your work, usually for the better.

That being the case, absorb the type of entertainment that you aspire to write. That way, you can gain the tools to continue advancing in your craft.

While taking in media can be a great way to recharge your creativity, there's also another simple thing that you can do to get yourself into the right headspace: *Nothing.*

That's right. Sometimes the best thing for an overworked brain is to turn off the critical thinking and do something mind-numbing. This can include activities such as playing video games, cards, putting together puzzles, walking, running, skating, sewing, drawing, or my current and most recent favorite activity, woodworking.

While you're working on these side projects and hobbies, you'll find that your mind is free to reorganize and refresh.

There are, however, dangers that come with taking breaks from the writing process.

# Losing The Flow

As authors, there are times when we get rolling and find that we're virtually unstoppable. Everything comes out perfectly well-constructed, the ideas flow like milk and honey, and we bang out thousands of words every day.

In that case, it's highly likely that you don't need to take a break. It might even be that taking a break will have the complete opposite effect of what you want it to have. It'll make you lose your rhythm.

Once that happens, you'll likely find that much more hard work and effort are required to get you back on track than what you managed to save up during your break. At that point, taking a break becomes not only pointless but counterproductive.

# Going Without

There's something else that you, as a creative individual, need to consider when it comes to taking a break: How long can you go without expressing yourself artistically? For many of us, writing, as well as creating in other formats, provides our lives with fulfillment and meaning. If you give it up for any length of time, be cognizant of the effect it will have on your psyche, on your subconscious self. If it begins to harm you, then immediately discontinue your break.

# Making A Career

There's one final topic that it would be good for you to factor into your decision of whether or not to take a break: Do you want writing to be a hobby or do you want it to be a career? If your answer is the former, then taking breaks won't have as great of a negative effect on you. You're writing for your self-fulfillment and enjoyment, and you don't need hard-set goals and writing schedules set in stone.

If your answer is the latter, though, if you want to make a career out of your writing, get published, sell articles, etc., then you need to be careful about taking breaks. To succeed in the writing industry, most authors need to be determined and self-motivated. They have to be able to meet the demands and deadlines of their dream job, or else that dream will always be just out of reach.

On top of that, the more you write, the more opportunities you have to succeed, to sell your articles, to get featured on a major blog, or to get a book contract with your dream publisher. Very few authors make a go of writing by working on one novel for ten to twenty years and then trying to pitch it around the world for another five to ten years.

By writing a novel a year, you'd be increasing your chances ten-fold, to say nothing of the first-hand experience and training that you'd gain from each completed project.

So, judge for yourself whether you need to take a break or not. Reflect on whether a break could improve, or impair, your progress as an author, and above all, always make sure that what you choose is the very best option for your well-being, as well as that of your loved ones.

# Writing Concepts—Character Archetypes

A character archetype is a typical character that appears over and over in literature, plays, television, and film. Character archetypes represent universal patterns of human nature.

As writers, these archetypes provide us with a method to understand our characters better, and to depict them accurately and authentically. They allow us to identify what motivates our characters and to flesh out how they would react in any given situation.

There are many different lists created by absolute geniuses in the fields of psychology that detail alternate versions of the character archetypes. Some of these lists contain eight different archetypes. Some of them contain twelve. Some of them contain a hundred.

It's not necessary to memorize all of the character archetypes that these experts have identified. Rather, these lists are meant to help give us as writers the resources we need to identify our characters, their habits, traits, and most probable courses of action.

One common character archetype is the mentor. A mentor provides the main character of a hero's journey with the information that they need to complete their quest. Often, a mentor will sacrifice themselves so that the hero can go on living, and, on the technical side of things, so that they have room to grow within the framework of the story. Well-known mentors include Obi-Wan Kenobi from *Star Wars IV: A New Hope*, Morpheus from *The Matrix*, Gandalf from *The Lord of the Rings*, and Albus Dumbledore from the *Harry Potter* franchise.

# Developing Your Character

*Basic Information > Location*

## Does his location affect the way others see him?

IF SO, WHY?

Deep prejudices can develop based on where a person or group may live. Characters may begin to feel and influence others into feeling that a person's location is representative of his social standing, his intelligence, or his capacity to succeed in a given venture. In *Snowpiercer*, an extreme class division develops between the various train cars and the individuals living within them. In *Total Recall* (2012), The United Federation of Britain looks down on the citizens of the Colony, considering them to be inferior, and using them as little more than slave labor for their ventures.

## How big is his home?

Generally, the better off a character is financially, the larger his home will be, although that convention might be bucked in the case of a rich character who takes a voluntary vow of poverty, who uses his riches for something other than gaining greater possessions, or who takes a journey of self-discovery. In *Batman*, Bruce Wayne invites Vicki Vale to his mansion for dinner and then jokes about the fact that the building is so large that he's never actually been in the room they're eating in.

## Does anyone else live with him?

Characters can live with their parents, their parents can live with them, or they can live with other family members, friends, roommates, or significant others. In *Friends*, Ross attempts to move in with Joey and Chandler but ends up irritating them to the point that they attempt to covertly convince him to leave. In *The Flash*, Iris and Barry Allen's future daughter moves into their apartment with the goal of getting to know her parents on a much more personal level.

## What is the condition of the outside of his home?

The outside of a character's home affects the opinions of everyone who passes by it. On the one hand, it can induce awe, admiration, and envy. On the other hand, it can foster disgust, fear, even hatred. In *Monster House*, Horace

Nebbercracker's house is old, dark, and decrepit. Its condition betrays the insidious nature of its history. In *The Lord of the Rings*, Frodo Baggins employs Samwise Gamgee as his gardener and groundskeeper. Samwise always makes sure that things are kept neat and tidy.

# Crafting Compelling Character Arcs—Black Widow

In *Avengers: Endgame*, Scarlett Johansson's character, Black Widow, chose to make the ultimate sacrifice to save the universe. Her selflessness won the day, providing the rest of the team with the tool they needed to restore billions of people back to life. While Black Widow's death was a tragic moment in the fourth *Avengers* film, if we look at it from a thematic viewpoint, we'd see that it was the only possible conclusion for her character arc.

In the world of storytelling, in the greatest of contrasts with the real world, every moment in a character's life is meant to be significant on a thematic level. By the time they reach their end destination, which may at times include their death, it's nearly a requirement that they complete a profound journey of character development.

While we are seldom provided with such perfect, rounded-off stories in the real world, this is an expectation for our novels, television series, and films. Some authors kill characters off indifferently and meaninglessly, but they are the exception, not the rule. If you choose to do this as a writer, it has to be a very informed and meaningful artistic choice on your part.

For the rest of us, Black Widow's sacrifice provides a perfect example of crafting compelling character arcs in our writing. What can we learn from the heroic choice that she makes in *Avengers: Endgame?*

In her second appearance in the Marvel Cinematic Universe (MCU), *Marvel's The Avengers*, Black Widow states that she has 'red in her ledger that she would like to wipe out,' a reference to the moral debts that she owes as a former mercenary, undoubtedly killing countless individuals.

Loki replies with the question, "Can you? Can you wipe out that much red?" In that back-and-forth exchange between these two characters, we get the foundation on which Black Widow's character development is based, as well as her core motivation. *She wants to make amends for past sins.*

A well-developed character arc would provide her with the opportunities to do just that, to show that she is willing to make sacrifices to balance out her moral debts. The corresponding scene in *Avengers: Endgame* gives us that moment in spades. She isn't satisfied with using her life to help others. Rather, when the time comes, she makes the choice to die so that millions can be saved.

This sacrifice comes at the conclusion of an emotional fight scene with her best friend, Hawkeye, who wants to make the same sacrifice that she is attempting to make. Black Widow owes her life to him. When he was sent to assassinate her, he saw the good in her and chose to cultivate it instead.

So Black Widow's death provides her character with the opportunity to repay the debt to her greatest friend, as well as the chance to completely wipe the symbolic red from her ledger. She completes a full, perfectly formed character arc, going from an indifferent killer to a guilty agent filled with regret, and finally to a self-sacrificing hero.

# Writing Definitions

## Caricature

A character with exaggerated and oversimplified features. In literature, this generally involves their personality and other attributes. It can be used for comedic effect or insult.

## Personification

A form of figurative language where non-human objects, animals, or ideas are given human characteristics. One example would be saying that the sun smiled.

## Anthropomorphism

Attributing human characteristics to animals or objects. It's different from personification because the latter is used to create imagery and poetic language, rather than making animals appear more human.

## Flanderization

The act of taking a single character trait and exaggerating it more and more over time until it completely consumes the character and becomes their defining characteristic. It is named after Ned Flanders from *The Simpsons*, who over the course of the show transforms from a well-rounded character to a caricature of himself.

## Character Agency

A character's ability to make decisions and affect the events of the story in meaningful ways. If a character doesn't have agency, then their story is at the very least not compelling, and at most dull and boring.

## Character Motivation

The reasons for why a character acts the way he does during a scene or throughout the story.

# December 23rd

The following articles were originally published in *The Writer's Everything*, Issue #008.

# The One-Week Author

Books, magazines, pamphlets, scrolls, clay tablets; the written word is a distinctly human invention. With it, we can share our thoughts, feelings, desires, and emotions across time and space. We can transfer our knowledge and wisdom directly to our readers' minds, achieving a level of intimate understanding that is unique to our species.

It's no wonder that millions of individuals around the world aspire to be authors. Unfortunately, however, this is a near-insurmountable goal for the vast majority of them. The ideas are there, as are the feelings and emotions they want to elicit in the hearts of their readers. But writing a book is an enormous undertaking that requires at least a moderate understanding of the art of storytelling.

If you look at the thickness of your favorite novel and despair at the thought of writing fifty to one hundred thousand words of your own, don't worry. An old adage asks, "How do you eat an elephant?" The answer, "One bite at a time."

It's totally within your power to chip away at your project, writing it little by little, word by word, developing your story over months, even years. The greatest thing you can do, however, comes before you even write *"Chapter One"* at the top of your page. The greatest thing you can do is prepare.

In one week, you can lay a firm foundation on which to build your novel. You can develop a course of action that can keep you pointed in the right direction no matter how long you find yourself writing. In one week, you can transform yourself from a dreamer to an author.

There may be 130 million books in the world, but the world doesn't have your book yet, and with a little bit of guidance and hard work, you can add your own unique perspective to the growing legacy of humankind.

# Day 1—Writing Utensils

If there's anything I've learned from my many years of trying to get back into weightlifting, it's that you shouldn't push yourself too hard on day one. I can't tell you how many first days I've spent pumping iron at the gym, only to be physically unable to bend my arms for the next week and a half.

So, in the same way, you want your transition to the

authorial mindset to be a gradual one. On day one, dedicate a few minutes to picking a writing utensil. Perhaps you might want to go out and buy a notebook and pen, something you can take with you wherever you go. Or maybe you might want to peruse the note-taking apps on the App Store, the Play Store, etc. Evernote, OneNote, iA Writer, Scrivener, Word, Pages... The options are nearly limitless.

It's never been a better time to be a writer. You can have access to the tools you need to work on your novel anywhere you need them, any time you want them. Once you've selected the appropriate writing utensils, give some thought to when you might want to pull them out and put words on the page.

Do you want to schedule certain amounts of time to write? Do you want to wake up early and knock out your writing goals? Do you want to work on your writing after work, or maybe before you go to sleep?

The most important thing is that you are at peak efficiency when you work on your writing. There's no point in waking up at 5 a.m. if you can't uncross your eyes before 7 o'clock. For me, waiting until right before bed to try to knock out a few articles or a couple thousand words in my latest novel is a complete waste. I've never fallen asleep quicker in my life than I do now that I'm trying to be productive with my evenings.

Once you've settled on a schedule, grab your writing utensil and write the date on the top. Write down what your goal for this book is, whether you want a certain word count, you want to have it done by a certain time, or whatever other goals you may have to help you accomplish this journey. Then, when you've reached the finish line, you can look back and see just how far you were able to go by setting your mind to the task.

# Day 2—Inspiration

Out of every step in this one-week journey to becoming an author, today's step, in my opinion, is the absolute most important one and should elicit the most time and effort on your part.

The best part of this step is that unless you live under a rock, with no access to televisions, theaters, smartphones, computers, bookshelves, or libraries, then you've more than likely already taken this essential step.

What step am I referring to?

Absorbing entertainment. If you want to add to the treasure-trove of stories that abound in the world, you need to know what some of those stories are. You especially need to know what your favorite stories are.

So, grab the writing utensils of your choice and make a list of your all-time favorite books, TV shows, movies, or video games. What do they all have in common?

The common denominators of your favorite pieces of entertainment are the very things that are going to inspire you through the rest of the writing process. If you love *Groundhog Day* and *Edge of Tomorrow*, then perhaps a repeating day story would be the perfect choice for you. If you love *Star Trek* and *Stargate*, then perhaps a space exploration story would be the perfect choice for you.

Be aware that this is not the time to force a story out of your head fully formed. You shouldn't be doing any planning or writing right now. If you happen to think of something, feel free to jot it down in the corner of your notebook, or on a separate file in your app, but otherwise, at this point, you simply want to access your brain's creativity, let it run wild, so that when it's time for you to start creating, you might find the first sprout of an idea already growing in your subconscious.

# Day 3—Parameters

Today is the day for you to start conceptualizing the parameters of your novel. This doesn't mean planning specific details of the story itself. We'll get to that later. Right now, what you need to do is form a picture of the end goal in your mind so that you can begin fitting the pieces in place. After all, piecing together a puzzle is much more difficult to do if you don't know what shape it is, what the picture is supposed to be, or which pieces belong to which puzzle.

For example, imagine that yesterday, you identified your love for heist stories. Today, you might extrapolate from that the need to have an ensemble cast with each individual specializing in a specific skill.

If you identified your love for hero stories, then it would be more likely that you would only have one main character, an individual who discovers a special ability or privilege that sets them apart from everyone else in the story.

If you identified your love for war stories, then the possibilities are endless. You can write a story about the futility and loss of war from the perspective of a soldier, you can write a story about the leaders of the war planning and executing their strategies, you can write a story about the civilians who are placed in harm's way, you can even write a story that covers the entirety of the war from beginning to end or even a story that extensively details the events of one specific battle or altercation.

This isn't the time to lock yourself into a story yet, and if you have multiple ideas, then write them all down on separate pages or in separate files. This step is simply meant to give you a firm foundation from which to push off.

Once you've finished establishing the parameters of your story, then go ahead and call it a day. Take the rest of the morning, afternoon, or evening off. Daydream about what your story could be. Let the creative juices flow freely. Tomorrow, you'll begin shaping your story.

# Day 4—Settings, Events, and Characters

Hopefully, you've had the chance to get in a little daydreaming. If not, then go ahead and put off your writing until a little bit later today, if it's convenient for you to do so. Creativity is the cornerstone of any novel, and cultivating it is one of the most important things you can do if you want to become a successful author.

Now that you've allowed your thoughts to run free and wild, we're going to start working on the really fun part of this process. We're going to be brainstorming events, settings, and characters.

This is the time for you to let your creativity take flight, to embrace the most enjoyable, exciting aspects of novel-writing. Now, we're going to talk about each of these three topics in order, but don't think that means that you have to tackle them in the same order, from settings to events to characters. Stories are like Chinese finger traps. You have to push everything into place at the same time to unlock their full potential.

A great number of stories will naturally lend themselves to one setting or another. If your story is about surviving an onslaught of poisonous serpents in close quarters, then your setting is going to need to be, by necessity, an enclosed space, one that you can't simply walk away from whenever the going gets tough, perhaps something like an airplane.

On the other hand, if your story is about two individuals falling in love, then the options for your setting are nearly limitless. From the Garden of Eden to the Roman Empire, from the Wild West to the 24th century, such a story is largely timeless.

*December 23rd*

In your writing utensil, place three words with spaces between them.

- Settings
- Events
- Characters

Once you've chosen your setting, write it in the appropriate blank space. Next to it, brainstorm a half dozen different ways that your setting might affect the plot of your story.

For example, if your story revolves around a couple starting a family in the Wild West, then infectious diseases and complications with childbirth will be very real threats for them.

Now write your complications down in the blank space next to your setting. These are what you're going to come back to if your story staggers or your creativity otherwise needs a boost.

Events will come to you as you picture your story more and more fully in your mind. If you're going to write a love story, then you might realize that you want to have the main heroine mistakenly believe that her love interest has done something terrible, one event, which leads her to remove him from her life, a second event, only to realize that she was mistaken the entire time, a third event. How is she going to correct her own mistakes? The answer to that question will form a fourth event, a fifth event, and more.

If you're going to write a fantasy story, then you might realize that you want the main character to find an item of great significance, one event. Then he's confronted by an old, wise man with a big, white beard, a second event. The man begins to train him in the use of the item, a third, a fourth, and maybe even a fifth event, until finally, the old man sacrifices himself so that the main character can escape certain doom, a sixth event.

If you can't picture more than one event at a time, don't worry about it. This isn't the point where you need to be stringing them all together, although it wouldn't hurt to start doing so if it comes naturally to you.

If you can't think of any events at all, that's understandable. We've been trained as a society to consume endless sources of media, but when asked what makes a good story, most people wouldn't know where to begin.

If you feel this way, then it's time to go back to your inspiration. If you have to, go as far as to borrow a few events from the stories you enjoy.

Did you like it when the army of robots attacked Del Spooner in *I, Robot*? Then maybe you can include in your list an event where a thousand robots all turn evil all at once. Did you like it when they uploaded kung fu directly into Neo's brain in *The Matrix*? Then maybe you can include an event where one of your characters has information uploaded into their brain.

Finally, we come to the characters. The people with whom you populate the pages of your novel are essential for the forward momentum of your story.

If Jean Valjean from *Les Misérables* had been bitten by a radioactive spider, to concoct an absurd premise, he would not have accepted the great responsibility that came with his great powers. Rather, he would have hidden out, working vigilantly not to bring attention to himself, just as he did in the aforementioned novel.

If Jane Bennet had caught the eye of Mr. Darcy in *Pride and Prejudice* rather than her sister Elizabeth, she would have never been so quick to judge his actions, and they would have never had a falling-out.

The single most important thing to keep in mind when choosing which characters fit in a given role is their motivation. If Thomas in *The Maze Runner* had been pessimistic, even suicidal, he never would have exerted the effort that he did to escape the maze and lead everyone to safety. If Jake Sully in *Avatar* had been wealthy and privileged, he never would have accepted the assignment to head to Pandora.

Once you've identified your characters, then begin filling in the blank space of your writing utensils with their descriptions. Especially keep in mind the ways they will affect and be affected by the story. What are their skills? What is it they need to achieve self-fulfillment? What is their fatal flaw? A well-crafted story will utilize all these aspects of its character to craft a compelling narrative around them.

Now, I know this seems like a big chunk of work to do all in one day, but that's the reason why the last few days were so easy in comparison. If you've taken the time to dwell on your inspirations, then ideally, there should be at least a few ideas that appear in your mind out of thin air, as if you were discovering them rather than creating them.

# Day 5—One-Sentence Premise

If you still felt like the tasks of day four were too complex, then today is the day to take things a little easier. We're going to focus on what your story is going to be about. Specifically, we're going to write a one-sentence premise for the plot of your novel.

This is the culmination of the last four days' work condensed into one compound sentence. To achieve this, you have to factor in everything you've already determined about your story. You have to do your best to imagine it as one whole, rather than separate, unrelated parts.

If over the course of this week thus far, you developed a modern-day setting, a killer robot, a time machine, and a woman being chased, then your one-sentence premise would be something like this: "What if there was a time-traveling robot sent to our modern-day world to kill people?"

If over the course of this week, you developed a space setting, a dark wizard, and a planet being blown up, then your one-sentence premise would be something like this: "What if an evil dark wizard uses a planet-destroying weapon to secure his rule?"

The one-sentence premise is the way you'd describe the bottom-line concept of your story. It should be boiled down to its simplest, purest form, and it should cover at least one-third of your novel.

In *The Terminator*, the premise of the time-traveling robot trying to kill the heroine lasts for roughly one-third of the movie, at which time she meets up with a soldier sent from the future to save her, and the premise transforms into: "The target of a time-traveling robot goes on the run with a man from the future as they attempt to destroy their murderous foe."

In *Star Wars IV: A New Hope*, the premise of an evil dark wizard using a planet-destroying weapon to secure his rule also lasts for roughly one-third of the movie, at which point the premise transforms into: "A young farmer must travel across the galaxy in search of the Rebellion, joining its ranks to destroy the Empire's arsenal and gain the upper hand on them."

Tomorrow, we will build that summary to include the other two-thirds of your story. For now, sit back, relax, and revel in the knowledge of how close you are to your goal of writing a novel.

# Day 6—One-Paragraph Premise

It's time to map out the other two-thirds of your story. For the one-paragraph premise, you're going to need to pull yourself back, as far away from the project as you can get, until you have a bird's-eye view of the entire story and all it encompasses.

This perspective is essential for making a coherent and meaningful story. It allows you to discover plot holes, illogical progressions of events, as well as to identify the theme and major story beats. It also allows you to make a simple, straightforward roadmap to guide you through the process of plotting out your novel.

Your one-paragraph premise needs to cover every major event in your story in terms that are as simple as you can make them.

For example, a one-paragraph premise of *Avatar* might go like this:

"A paraplegic veteran agrees to go on a dangerous mission in a far-away world in exchange for spinal surgery. He soon realizes the situation on the planet isn't as cut-and-dry as he would like, and the closer he grows to the natives, the harder it is for him to continue with his assignment. Finally, he chooses to refuse his orders and save the natives from destruction. In the ensuing battle, they defeat the humans, forcing them off the planet, and he transfers into his avatar body permanently."

A one-paragraph premise of *Iron Man* might go like this:

"A wealthy weapons manufacturer is captured by terrorists and forced to build missiles for them. Instead, he creates a tactical suit of armor with which he gains his freedom. Upon returning home, he discovers that the head of his company is crooked, selling weapons to terrorists, and he makes it his goal to right those wrongs. Finally, he confronts the head of the company, who stole his technology and made a suit of his own. In the ensuing battle, he defeats his former mentor."

Keep it simple and straightforward.

Also, your main character should follow an arc, starting with their want, the thing that they think will make them happy, such as Jake Sully's healed legs in *Avatar*. Then they realize that there's something more important than what they want, such as Tony Stark's mission to stop the underhanded dealings at his company in *Iron Man*. Finally, they fully embrace the change, often, but not always, giving up their want in the process.

We have one day left, and it's a fun one. So, rest up, and prepare for your final day of novel-writing preparation.

# Day 7—Plotting Like An Excited Seven-Year-Old

Here we go. We've made it to day seven. You've almost finished your novel preparation. You're just about to lay out the last domino that, when pushed, will lead inexorably to your goal.

Today's task is a big one, but also a fun one. I like to call it, "Plotting like an excited seven-year-old." If your son, daughter, niece, nephew, grandson, granddaughter, or the like, were to watch a movie and summarize it to you, what would it be like?

Children are so full of excitement and energy when they're talking about a movie they enjoy, and that's how you need to be on day seven. That excitement will help you to complete this task, even if you're an ardent pantser, someone who dislikes preparing outlines before writing.

Imagine a seven-year-old explaining *Titanic* to you.

"Ok, ok, so first this guy is playing some game, and he like wins, and then he gets on a big boat, and he meets this girl. They hang out for a while and look at naughty drawings, and then they eat at some fancy restaurant and dance together.

Then, um, well my mommy covered my eyes, but then the ship runs into a big piece of ice!"

You don't have to include all the oks and the ands, and you don't have to censor yourself, but the point is that this is the opportunity to highlight all the exciting moments that made you so eager to tell this story in the first place. This summary is your roadmap to guide you through the entirety of your novel-writing process.

# The One-Week Author

At this point, you're in one of two categories. On the one hand, you've finished this quick, straightforward program, and you're well on the way to achieving your dream of becoming an author. On the other hand, you've just read through the entire guide, and now you're ready to start with day one.

Either way, allow me to congratulate you. You've taken the first step to the fun, rewarding, and unforgettable experience of writing your own novel. For people like us, this is one of the most meaningful things we can do with our creativity. This is one of the most successful ways we can share our voice with the world. I can't wait to enjoy yours.

# Writing Concepts—Character Wants

A character arc, something that we all want to include if we intend for our stories to have deep, significant consequences on our main characters and meaning for our readers, is essentially a transition from what a character wants to what a character needs.

Character wants are the starting point for any character arc with the exception of flat arcs, in which the character and his wants remain the same throughout the story.

Generally, the things the character wants are either selfish and self-centered, or in some other way not compatible with their achieving a sense of purpose and fulfillment in life.

This is especially true with the positive character arc, where the character transitions into a better version of themselves by the end of the story. In *Shrek*, the titular protagonist starts with the desire to be left alone in his swamp. That's his self-centered need that he has to learn to look past to imbue his life with meaning.

In negative character arcs, we often find the opposite character progression demonstrated. The character starts as the best, or at least a better, version of themselves, and throughout the story, they are influenced by events and the characters they interact with to develop negative qualities. In *1984*, Winston Smith begins the story with wants that include freedom from the oppressive regime in power, but by the end of the story, he's been brainwashed into loving the ruling class.

# Developing Your Character

*Basic Information > Location*

## What is the condition of the inside of his home?

The condition of the inside of a character's home can reveal deep aspects of his personality. Perhaps he's organized and likes to have everything in its place. Perhaps he's obsessive, freaking out if a single item is knocked out of line. Or perhaps he is lazy, having little to no desire to clean and maintain his home. In *The Big Bang Theory*, Leonard and Sheldon live in a state of organized chaos, while Penny's apartment is nothing short of pure, messy disorganization. In the *Iron Man* series, Tony Stark is very obsessive about having everything in his house organized just right, even going as far as to make a big deal over the location of a giant stuffed rabbit.

## Does he like his home?

Some characters may thrive in conditions in which others would simply be unable to function. On top of that, homes can come in a wide variety of sizes and styles. While one character may love a spartan, one-bedroom flat, another may be unable to function in a house of fewer than three bedrooms. In *The Big Bang Theory*, Penny functions best when her apartment is a mess because she knows the location of every item in it. Sheldon, however, can barely stand being in her apartment, and even goes as far as to break in late at night to organize it without Penny's knowledge or permission.

## Do others like his home?

The condition of a character's home can have far-reaching effects on their social standing in the eyes of others, as well as their interactions with them. A neat, tidy, well-furnished home may attract many visitors, even freeloaders, while a messy, unorganized, trash-laden home would keep all but the closest of friends at bay. In *The Big Bang Theory*, Sheldon is incapable of putting up with the disorganized state of Penny's apartment, and he even goes so far as to take it upon himself to organize it for her.

## Where does he wish he lived?

It is very common for characters to wish that they could be somewhere other than where they currently are, regardless of whether they like or dislike their home, and regardless of whether it is a home that others envy, or one they detest. In *The Lord of the Rings*, both Bilbo, and eventually Frodo, realize that the Shire is too slow-paced for them, and they decide to journey with the elves to the other side of the sea. In *La La Land*, Mia Dolan moves to Los Angeles for the sole purpose of pursuing her dream of becoming an actress.

# Crafting Compelling Character Arcs—Iron Man

In *Avengers: Endgame*, Tony Stark utters the now-iconic words that first opened the door eleven years earlier to the flood of record-breaking content that is the Marvel Cinematic Universe (MCU).

What were they?

"I am Iron Man."

If you've seen the movie, you know exactly what scene I'm speaking of, as well as what a profound and moving moment it truly is.

If we look at it from a thematic standpoint, however, we find that it is more than just an emotional and heart-wrenching end to a three-hour-and-two-minute action extravaganza. It was the conclusion to a deep, meaningful, well-crafted character arc.

To fully understand the significance of the final act of one of the greatest superhero films of all time, we have to go back to his debut appearance in *Iron Man*.

# The Starting Point

In this introductory film, Tony Stark is depicted as egotistical and self-centered. He's too busy having a good time to bother accepting an award from his best friend, and when a journalist calls him out on his shady business practices, he chooses to seduce her to his bedroom rather than face the truth of her statements.

Tony Stark is the type of person who will always put himself first. The idea of sacrificing himself for anyone else doesn't even cross his mind. That is the starting point of his character arc.

# The First Step

Tony Stark takes the first step towards his profound development as a character when the convoy that he is riding in is attacked by an extremist group, the Ten Rings. They demolish Tony Stark's Humvee with his own missiles, capture him, and force him to build more weapons for them lest they kill him.

At that moment, the concerns that he had shrugged off so easily in the previous scene, concerns about his business practices, become very real and very significant to him personally.

This is not, however, the turning point for Tony Stark as a character, the moment where he transitions from pursuing his wants to working towards his needs. Rather, that moment comes next.

## The Turning Point

Up until Tony's escape from the cave in which he was being held captive, his goals were still wholly self-centered. He wanted to free himself from captivity and get back to his old life. The needs that his character would come to discover were nowhere on his radar.

But then he develops a friendship with Professor Yinsen. Yinsen sees past Tony Stark's facade, realizing that he, with a little effort, has the potential to be a great man. Their friendship is the turning point that sets Tony Stark on the path to redemption.

## Don't Waste Your Life

As Tony Stark's prototype Iron Man armor is charging up, much too slowly for him to stop the terrorists at his door, Yinsen decides to sacrifice himself. He runs out with a machine gun, creating the distraction Stark needs to be able to get his suit operational.

Yinsen's dying words to Stark are a plea: "Don't waste your life." Yinsen put his faith in Tony. He demonstrates the belief that Stark's life is worth more than his own, and it is that sacrifice, that confidence, that forms the driving force behind everything Tony Stark then does as Iron Man.

## Teetering On The Edge

In the early days of his newfound career as a superhero, we find Tony Stark teetering on the edge. One foot is behind him, planted firmly in the safety of his old life, his old aspirations, and his old ideals. The other foot is hovering above a ravine, the selfless, self-sacrificing, self-fulfilling life that he never realized he needed.

It isn't until his mentor, Obadiah Stane, steals his technology for his own selfish ends that Tony Stark finally takes the leap, learning to fly, metaphorically speaking. When presented with the chance to put his old arc reactor back in his chest and save himself, leaving Stane to his evil endeavors, he chooses to confront Stane. By the time the battle reaches its climax, he heroically and selflessly chooses to stop his enemy at the cost of his own life.

# Not The End

This, of course, is the conclusion to Tony Stark's character arc in *Iron Man*. It is not, however, the end of his character development in the MCU. Throughout his next eight appearances, he struggles with making the best choices in his new position as a hero and, later, a leader and mentor.

In *Marvel's The Avengers*, Captain America calls Iron Man out for not being willing to make the sacrifice play, as well as for being nothing without his suit. In *Avengers: Age of Ultron*, Iron Man unintentionally creates a malicious, rogue A.I. in his attempt to protect the world. Then, his overreaction to his own mistake leads to the split and near destruction of the Avengers.

With each appearance, however, we see his pride and vanity being slowly chipped away until he reaches his final chronological appearance in *Avengers: Endgame* and his character arc comes full circle.

# A Fitting Conclusion

Tony Stark goes into the battle with Thanos knowing that there is only one possible solution. Even so, he is not aware of the sacrifice play that their current course of action will require him to make.

Finally, the time comes, Doctor Strange signals him, reminding him that this is the moment of truth, and Tony Stark acts. He shows us all exactly who he is, using the infinity stones to save the universe in spite of the deadly effect of his wielding them.

In his dying moment, the script shows us that he looks to Pepper Potts, the words "I'm sorry" crossing his mind before he breathes his last breath. He has fully embraced his character needs. He's performed a transformation, a complete, one-hundred and eighty-degree turn-around.

He is no longer egotistical and self-centered. He no longer puts himself first with no regard for others. What matters to him are his friends, his family, and the universe, and he has them all at the forefront of his mind, even in his dying moment.

A truly outstanding example of a terrific character arc achieving a wonderful, touching, and fitting conclusion.

# Writing Definitions

## Archetype

An ideal or typical example. An archetype is a pattern that you can use to help develop and understand your characters. Different archetype systems identify characters in different ways.

## Iconic Character

Characters that stand out from, and elevate, the stories they are in. They're characters you love to spend time with and with whom you wish you could continue to do so long after the stories are done. They are not necessarily the main characters.

## Character Arc

The transformation of a character throughout the story, pictured as a line arching across a graph. There can be positive, negative, and flat arcs, depending on the state of the character at the end of the story.

# Positive Character Arc

A character arc in which the character improves as a person throughout the story. That is to say, they start the story with negative qualities or beliefs, and gradually shed them. An example would be Ebenezer Scrooge from *A Christmas Carol.*

# Negative Character Arc

A character arc in which the character starts with positive qualities or beliefs, and gradually loses them, becoming a worse person by the end of the story. An example would be Anakin Skywalker in the *Star Wars* prequel trilogy.

# Flat Character Arc

A character arc in which the character stays the same throughout the story, but generally tends to influence the world around them because of their firmly held beliefs. An example would be Indiana Jones in the film *Raiders of the Lost Ark.*

# Bonus Essay: Discovering Inspiration

This essay is part one of a series that was offered to the Kickstarter supporters of my upcoming character development guide, *If So, Why?*

Everyone dreams of being an author. The desire to tell stories is all but engrained into our DNA. Yet even with that being the case, writing doesn't necessarily come naturally for most of us. Why is that?

Part of the reason may be that there are simply so many steps to writing a novel, and to be successful in your endeavors, you must be able to transition from one to the next to the next almost seamlessly.

You have to develop your characters, plan their arcs, plan the theme, plan the plot, write an outline, write a first draft, revise your first draft—the list goes on. Writing a novel is a long and arduous process, and every step is just as important as the next in your work's success.

There is one step, however, that is far and away the most essential part of the creative process. Without succeeding in this step, the rest of your efforts will implode in on themselves, leaving you with the steaming wreckage of an unsuccessful novel.

This step at first may sound like it's passive. You may wonder if it's even possible to actually *take* this step. But the truth is that there are many options that lead to your achieving it.

The step, of course, is discovering inspiration.

This may be the point where you interject. "I don't need to discover inspiration. I'm *already* sufficiently inspired."

So why am I still going to insist that you need to put forth added effort in this regard?

# The Need For Inspiration

As a writer, you need inspiration for every single step in the process of creating a novel. From coming up with ideas, to crafting your characters, to developing their arcs, to building their world, to structuring your novel, proper inspiration is a necessity.

It's true. Inspiration seems to come naturally to some of us. You may feel that your subconscious is brimming with ideas. There's a never-ending barrage of them shooting past your conscious mind in your every waking moment.

While that may be true for you now, it might not always be the case. As unfortunate as it is, there are reasons why we may begin to feel less creative than we used to.

Part of this may be due to age. While children on the playground can imagine epic battles of good versus evil playing out on a planetary scale, adults can't seem to imagine anything other than how many past due notices they're going to get in the mail this morning.

For others, the constant act of being overloaded with work, responsibilities, and especially stress may sap the creativity right out of you.

Even if you have the full faculty of your creativity, and you take advantage of it, you may find that it's a limited resource. Just like going on a road trip with a tank full of gas, you'll eventually find a little blinking light on your dashboard signaling that your road trip is about to come to a premature stop.

Unfortunately, if any of these situations are the case for you, you'll find it near impossible to have success as a writer. So, what's the fix? How can you discover inspiration?

## Discovering Inspiration

Put simply, you need to stop expelling your creativity and start absorbing it, stockpiling it. It sounds easy, but in truth, it's far from it.

We don't live in a world that caters to writers. There's a reason why everyone's heard of "starving artists". Every single one of us, save the extremely fortunate, must work to make a living, to pay the rent, to provide for ourselves and our families, and to live up to social expectations.

It's very rare in the midst of all these demands on your time and energy that you will have the opportunity to just stop and catch your breath. Yet that is exactly what you need to do.

Now, it's worth noting before we begin that not all things inspire all people equally. The Greek myths that cause me to dream of histories long past or duties yet to come may be nothing more than meaningless drivel to you. On the other hand, the success story of an up-and-coming college football player may drive you to write a profound success story of your own, while all the while, I'm over here going on about how much I hate sports.

We all have to discover what inspires us. We have to find our own muses. But having a place to begin will always be helpful, no matter who we are.

It's a long and complex journey trying to discover inspiration, but with a little guidance, and a point for you to push off from, you can succeed in doing so. So, let's look at four essential steps you can take in your struggle to discover inspiration.

# Absorbing Entertainment

Absorbing entertainment is one of the most essential steps that a storyteller can take. After all, if you want to add to the wealth of stories that exist in the world, you need to have an idea of what some of those stories are.

Many scoff at the idea of basing their creative focus on the works of other authors. They feel that it hinders their creativity, putting unwanted constraints on their work. However, there are three good reasons why you should look to the stories of others for inspiration.

1.  It helps you to discover what your audience is expecting. Every genre comes with certain "genre conventions," things that readers expect to see from these types of stories. These are the things that make the stories feel whole. Abiding by these genre conventions may sound limiting, but what it means is that you're gaining insight into what your audience wants to see happen in your work. If you want to be successful, you have to do at least a little... well, I'm not going to call it pandering, but you get the idea.
2.  It gives you a jump-start on your craft. Looking at the

works of others can help you to skip past the awkward, unsure experimental stage of your writing, and learn key techniques for crafting excellent stories. No one considers a painter to be a fraud just because he learned a lesson about the use of colors from Van Gogh, or the depiction of depth from Da Vinci. In the same way, learning writing techniques from other authors and writers does not make you a phony author.

3.  It allows you to advance the development of our culture and society. Sure, I wouldn't blame you if you accused me of being a little lofty and high-minded on this one. However, take just a moment to give this some consideration. Would *Game of Thrones* or *Harry Potter* exist if it weren't for J.R.R. Tolkien? Would *2001: A Space Odyssey* or *Star Trek* exist without H.G. Wells? Humanity is nothing more than one huge collaboration, and the results are ongoing. By familiarizing yourself with the works that have come before your own, you have the opportunity to build off of them and add to our ever-evolving legacy.

So how do we absorb entertainment? Well, the best part of this step is that unless you live under a literal rock, you're more than likely already doing it. We are inundated by a virtual flood of entertainment, good and bad, from movies and television to novels and podcasts.

Your entire life is an experiment in discovering what sorts of stories appeal to you as an individual. After all, you aren't going to waste your time on entertainment you don't like.

So, make a list of all your personal favorites. As you do so, try to look for the common denominators among them. What is it they all have in common? Do they all include time travel? Polar opposite characters who fall madly in love? A character unjustly accused of crimes he didn't commit? Once you know what it is that you enjoy the most in other stories, you'll have a checklist of sorts for your own stories.

Again, though, the goal is to collaborate with humanity. So, you can't just settle for replicating or rehashing all of your favorites. Instead, try to build off of them in new and surprising ways. Offer the world something new, something from your own unique perspective.

That's step one. How are you feeling so far? Are you comfortably analyzing your entertainment, looking to pick up on the details, both large and small, that you can use for your own story?

Good, because the next step flies in the face of everything I just said.

# The Sound of Silence

You're going to start this exercise the same way that you'll end it. That is by doing *nothing*. Now, I know, I know. It seems counterintuitive. However, taking a simple, quiet, relaxing breather away from everything can be incredibly refreshing and unbelievably beneficial to your creativity.

Doing nothing allows you to collect your thoughts. Instead of a constant barrage of sensory input, you're giving your brain the freedom to wander about aimlessly.

I believe that for most people, our brains are hardwired for creativity. Virtually every child in preschool has just as much fun as the rest of them when it comes to drawing with a crayon or stacking blocks into the rough shape of a castle.

More often than not, if you set your brain free, it will naturally do whatever it can to fill the void you've provided in order to entertain you. You'll find yourself following along in the back seat of your mind's eye as it leads you to some of the most creative ideas you've ever had.

The problem with this step, unfortunately, is obvious.

*Bonus Essay: Discovering Inspiration*

It's not easy in our modern world for us to just sit down and do nothing. Unlike our ancestors, who looked up at the starry night sky with wonder, we're busy looking at our cell phones with indifference.

There's a reason why so many young children eventually give up drawing. Their free time ends up being filled with all the numerous sources of entertainment at their disposal. They get caught up in consuming media.

Now-a-days, consuming media is just what we do. It's like we've been programmed for it. If we're not listening to a podcast, we're watching Netflix. If we're not watching Netflix, we're playing video games. If we're not playing video games, we're checking our Twitter feed.

What can we do to solve this problem, to give our brains a rest, to allow them the freedom they need in order to create? We need to examine all the situations where we consume media and cut them down drastically.

Be careful not to eliminate them completely, though. Being entertained is vitally important in our lives, and as authors, there are so many sources we can look to for help in building our craft.

There are audiobooks and podcasts that teach us the art of

164

writing. There are books, movies, and television shows that give us an incredible amount of insight into the methodology of storytelling.

So there certainly needs to be a balance between these first two steps if you want to get the greatest benefit from your books, movies, television shows, and podcasts. By combining these steps, you'll be able to land a quick one-two punch to knock out even the toughest of writer's block.

But there's an even better way to get yourself in the creative mindset.

## Keep A Journal

If you want to be a storyteller, what better experience is there than telling your own stories while the events are still fresh in your mind?

As a writer, it's basically in your job description to pull from your own life. This, of course, doesn't mean that you have to be a gladiator, a space-ship captain, or a super-spy. It doesn't mean that your uncle has to have betrayed your father to his death, that you have to have been locked in a tower for as long as you can remember, or that you have to have been caught in an epic love story that could end no other way than with your demise.

What it does mean is that you extrapolate the stories of your characters from your own experiences. You take your history, thoughts, and emotions and graft them into the lives of your characters.

Our lives are brimming with experiences, large and small. They provide us with data, emotions, and information that allows us to write meaningful, resonating stories.

The more you write about your life, your own story, the easier it will become to write about the story of others. The more you write about your feelings and emotions, the more you can relate to the feelings and emotions of your characters.

It's so important for you as an author to connect to your characters on an emotional level. They need to become real to you if you want to have any hope of realistically creating them and their world.

There's another source beyond your day-to-day life that makes for fantastic material for your journaling efforts. What is it? Your subconscious. Many people write in what they refer to as dream journals, cataloguing the epic adventures they participate in every time they go to sleep.

Now, I have to admit, this isn't an option for everyone. I've encountered many people who state in no uncertain terms that they never remember a single dream. They usually describe this with the words, "I don't dream," but the truth relates to their memory rather than the act itself.

There are methods for alleviating this problem, but they usually require you to take some fairly inconvenient steps, such as setting an alarm for some god-forsaken hour of the morning with the goal of pulling you into consciousness in the middle of your dreams. Personally, I'd choose the sleep over the dream journal every time.

However, if you are the type of person that can remember your dreams, in whole or in part, then by all means, you should take full advantage of it.

Dreams are the purest expression of creativity your mind can muster. They're wild and crazy and random and they make no sense whatsoever, yet still manage to resonate with you on a profoundly emotional level. The potential of your dreams is limitless, and within them you can find ideas that you never would have discovered relying solely on your rational mind.

I'm fortunate enough to remember my dreams in great detail. I've even been able to control them at times to the extent that I can keep the narrative going, providing me with more and more interesting concepts. In fact, the first book of my adult life was written nearly word for word from the events of a vivid dream in which I was attempting to survive the zombie apocalypse.

Don't think, though, that that's the only way you can find inspiration from your dreams. Every moment, event, and situation that you dream about has the potential to be reshaped into the narrative of your novel.

Were you being chased by shape-shifting aliens that turned into clowns and then started having tea with you before burping the alphabet? In that case, perhaps you could write a story about shape-shifting aliens.

Don't feel like you have to use all of your dream, and especially don't feel like your dreams have to make perfect sense before you can adapt them into your story. Instead, pick and choose events and situations to adapt into your novel, and adapt your own meanings from the chaos.

This is equally true of any of your journal entries, whether about dreams, your day-to-day life, or even something more creative, like a stream-of-consciousness list of ideas.

Save the events in your journal. If you ever find yourself in need of a good idea, if you ever find yourself lacking inspiration all together, then take those journal entries and use them as a jumping off point.

All of these suggestions, however, are useless if you don't do the following.

# Live Your Life

As writers, being introverts is basically our job description. Sure, this might not always hold true for everyone, but for the most part, we'd rather sit in the corner of a quiet house reading, or writing, a good book, as opposed to spending a night on the town.

Yet there comes a point where staying home and reading or writing about life just isn't enough. Now don't think I'm trying to tell you to "get a life!" Rather, what I'm saying is that the more life you've lived, the more inspiration you'll have for your writing.

Making the choice to be adventurous every once in a while will give you the experiences you need to fill your journal. It will provide fuel for more and more epic encounters in your dreams. And it will familiarize you with the wide range of emotions that you will have to represent in your characters.

*Bonus Essay: Discovering Inspiration*

A highly shared, highly repeated rule of writing is to write what you know. As I've already made clear, this doesn't mean that you have to be a gladiator, a space-ship captain, or a super-spy. But you do have to have experiences from which you can extrapolate the adventures of your characters.

The more you do, the more you experience, the more you can write. As your knowledge of the world and its history expands, so does the scope of your stories.

There's a good reason why preteens only write stories about preteen protagonists. That is the extent of their life experience. They lack the depth of experiences required in order to extrapolate the characteristics of a high schooler, a college student, or a parent.

You can't just spend your whole life holed up somewhere. You need to be part of the world that you wish to replicate. You need to interact with the humans that you wish to depict. You do that, and the inspiration will come naturally.

## Fill Up The Tank

As you go through these steps in an effort to discover your own inspiration, be sure to keep one thing in mind: your goal with each and every one of these steps is to take in, to absorb. Don't force yourself into the creating mode while you're still trying to refill your creativity.

If you're on a cross-country road trip and your gas needle is hovering over the E, it wouldn't do any good to put 30 cents worth of gas into it and then take off again. That would only leave you stranded far from your destination.

So, take your time. Fill up your tank.

If some ideas come naturally to you during the process, don't be afraid to jot them down. You should obviously never pass up or turn away a good idea. But your focus isn't to create.

That comes later.

Discover your inspiration. Refuel your creativity. If you do, then by the time you actually sit down to write, you'll discover the ideas flying by at breakneck speeds as you put the pedal to the metal.

And trust me when I tell you that you'll never have a greater time writing.

# My Works and Links

## *Chronicles of the Infected*

*Those They Betrayed*

## *The Writer's Everything*

*qjmartin.org/twe*

## *The Writer's Everything Quarterly*

*01: October—December 2019*
*02: January—March 2020*

## *Join My Newsletter*

*qjmartin.org/newsletter*

## *Support My Writing*

*patreon.com/qjmartin*